Inhale the present.
Exhale the future.

# the MINDFUL
# STARTUP

a wholehearted guide
through the mindful and compassionate
entrepreneurial journey

## Malte Krohn

www.onmindsandmotion.com/the-mindful-startup

LinkedIn: krohnmalte

First Edition.

ISBN 978-3-00-070172-6

Every effort has been made to contact copyright holders of material used in this product. The author apologizes for any error and would be grateful if notified of any corrections that should be incorporated in subsequent reprints or editions of this book.

Text and visualizations by Malte Krohn.

Cover design by Anna-Lena Krohn, Pia-Rosa Schäfer and Malte Krohn

Typesetting and layout by Anna-Lena Krohn.

Illustrations by Pia-Rosa Schäfer and Anna-Lena Krohn.

Printed by Lightning Source LLC,1246 Heil Quaker Blvd., LaVergne, TN. 37086, USA

## Disclaimer

This book is by no means intended to be a substitute for any medical advice or treatment. Any person with a condition or circumstances that require medical attention should reach out to a qualified therapist or medical practitioner.

Furthermore, the methods and practices in this book are carefully selected and described. They reflect commonly accepted approaches. However, performing these methods and practices is ultimately the reader's own responsibility. The author shall not be held responsible to any entity or person for any respective loss or consequential damage caused or alleged to be caused, whether directly or indirectly by the information provided in this book.

# The Journey

# Your Companion

In a way, you could consider this a romantic novel. No, you didn't pick up the wrong book... It tells the story of two isolated strings of events in my life, which eventually started to connect in late 2018.

While this is definitely not an autobiography, you should at least know the basic plot of this romance. Not to understand me but to understand the origins of my message. It emerged from my own experience and even more importantly, from the bottom of my heart. Let me briefly share how I got here.

Over the last twelve years, I have dedicated my studies, my personal time and my ongoing PhD research to understanding and driving change through entrepreneurship and innovation. I started exploring the craft of innovation during my bachelor studies in product development. However, it bothered me to have such a limited technology-centered perspective. So, I set out for a broader view and, during my MSc. in Global Innovation Management, I learned to look at innovation from a management perspective. Taking this forward, I joined the management team of Hamburg University of Technology's MSc. in Global Technology and Innovation Management & Entrepreneurship for a while. Finally, my industry-based PhD gives me a unique opportunity to put my perspectives into action in a four-year business model innovation project. I am currently finalizing the academic reflection on this project, in which I am applying the tools of social psychology to explore the role of people's mindsets with regard to innovation. Lastly, during the last few years, I mentored student teams in the University Innovation Fellows program of Stanford University's d.school at Hamburg University of Technology. In this role, I observed how students' passion, grit and personal agency are empowered by human-centered approaches to innovation and consequently create sustainable change. During my journey, I always tried to put humans at the center of my mission to empower changemakers.

However, this is only one part of my story. When I was 11 years old, my friend Dominik took me to my first ever Tae Kwon Do session. Three years later, in 2002, I was awarded my black belt. I was hooked, and I dedicated many years to my martial arts practice, resulting in titles at regional and national level Kung Fu competitions between 2006 and 2012. For the last ten years or so, my practice has focused on more gentle disciplines like *Yoga* and soft acrobatics. I am a Yoga Alliance certified *Vinyasa Yoga* teacher with The Peaceful Warriors and I completed a Thai Yoga Massage training with my friend and teacher Lucie Beyer. Following my mentor and kindred spirit Merlin Lang, I aim to integrate my insights into a holistic, mindful movement practice. My greatest fascination in this field was always with the connection between body and mind. So, in 2020 I took part in an eight-week *Mindfulness Based Stress Reduction* training with The

Mindful Spaces in Hamburg (you will read much more about this experience in Chapter 6).

Things got interesting when I met my PhD supervisor Professor Cornelius Herstatt after he came back from his holiday at the end of 2018. Well, at least I believed it had been a holiday. It turned out that he had just completed a Yoga teacher training. I was fascinated by the experiences he shared, and almost surprised that it had never occurred to me to do the same. Long story short, in January 2019 I went off to Bali for five weeks and underwent a teacher training myself. Of course, I experienced a substantial post-training life crisis... What am I doing with my time? What do I really want? What do I bring into this world?

You might not be surprised to hear that Yoga teacher training graduates frequently quit their jobs and fundamentally change their life. It wasn't that extreme for me. However, I did start to question certain things. Then, in March 2019, I was very privileged to be invited to the University Innovation Fellows Silicon Valley Meetup. This event brings together newly-trained fellows and their faculty mentors for several days of immersive learning activities. It takes place at Stanford University's d.school, and includes visits to Google and other Silicon Valley locations. Some of these experiences opened my eyes in a different way. Google's *chief innovation evangelist* Frederik Pferdt introduced the concept of psychological safety and actually did a loving-kindness meditation with us. Aleta Hayes, dance teacher at Stanford, guided an intense movement workshop, which stressed the importance of human connection and our own sense of self-worth. Believe it or not, I had a deeply spiritual experience at this workshop. Even more importantly, I realized I could potentially integrate my previously separated paths.

So, I believe that my two perspectives can actually be integrated into a powerful synergetic one. Why would that matter to you? The purpose of the rest of this book is to explain that. For now, I want to stress that this world needs changemakers. We need ideas, innovation, and most importantly purpose-driven entrepreneurs who take on the challenges of our global society.

However, as a society, we are not asking for a small favor. Driving change means ambiguity, it means hard work and it means stepping out of our comfort zone. While tackling the external challenge of developing ideas and creating a viable business, entrepreneurs are also dealing with tough "internal challenges". In this book, I want to share some of the latest scientific findings, plus my own vision on how to successfully deal with all this and truly create the future from the present moment. To turn this book into a shared journey, each chapter includes exercises that might give you a nudge into your present moment or closer to your own path of mindful change. Moreover, five chapters include conversations with experts who share their own personal stories and wisdom.

Hoping that I can open up potential ways for more people in the world to create the future from the present moment, I dedicate this book to:

- Aspiring entrepreneurs who want to take important mindfulness skills and innovation tools into their entrepreneurial journey

- Entrepreneurs and changemakers who are constantly giving 110% and already know they can't sustain this way of driving change, or who simply want to become more effective in what they are doing

- Educators, entrepreneurship training facilitators and coaches who want to empower their protégés to drive purposeful change in a more fulfilling way

- Ecosystem builders who want to facilitate mindful human-centered innovation and sustainable change

If this resonates with you, feel free to join this moment-to-moment journey into a purposeful future. If it doesn't, you are still welcome to give it a try, and maybe I can ignite a spark in your heart that you don't yet even know exists.

Thank you for taking a moment to learn where I am coming from. Now, let's start this journey of *Entrepreneurial Mindfulness* together.

"God, give me grace to accept with serenity the things that cannot be changed, courage to change the things which should be changed, and the wisdom to distinguish the one from the other."

REINHOLD NIEBUHR

# Embarking on Our Journey

It was curiosity that got me here and you might be curious, too. Perfect, we are already in this together! "What is a mindful startup?" — you might ask; and you would be right to do so! For now, I want to give you a head start by keeping this simple and straightforward. Eric Ries' book *The Lean Startup* turned the world of entrepreneurs and ventures upside-down. In my opinion, it is still one of the most important startup books out there. So, why reinvent the wheel? Eric Ries suggests that a startup is a specific type of business venture.[1] In his view, startups are human endeavors that can be characterized by two main criteria. First, they are created to develop and market new services or products. Second, they act under *conditions of extreme uncertainty*. His approach is widely applied in the startup world, so his criteria arguably serve their purpose. However, it does not touch on the mindfulness part. There are a few challenges for our society and entrepreneurs that, in my humble opinion, need some more attention: namely, the types of products and services that startups create and the way humans are involved in these ventures. Eric Ries points it out quite bluntly himself – conditions of extreme uncertainty. Of course, we will have a much closer look at this environment later on. At this point, I want to propose that we consciously address these conditions and take better care of our changemakers. I envision a global entrepreneurial ecosystem that allows founders to mindfully navigate startups' inherent conditions of extreme uncertainty in a way that allows them to take their whole selves on a fulfilling entrepreneurial journey. I would also like to see a global entrepreneurship community that supports more startups to deliver products and services that serve a socially or sustainability-driven purpose.

I feel like we got so lost in hype about AI, machine learning and other technologies that we forgot a simple fact – the most crucial and complex technology any entrepreneur has to master is their own mind. I believe that this can only happen if changemakers venture into their journey with Entrepreneurial Mindfulness.

The credit for this term belongs to Humera Fasihuddin, co-founder of the amazing University Innovation Fellows program (which will be mentioned many times, so you'd best get used to it). Earlier the year, when I started to write this book, we had a conversation about the challenges of aspiring changemakers and she proposed an *Entrepreneurial Mindfulness Meetup*. While the event, which might or might not be held in Hamburg, is yet to be created, my mind was ignited by the term Entrepreneurial Mindfulness itself. Fast forward to today, I started my venture of making Entrepreneurial Mindfulness a "thing" and the d.school accepted it as a project, run by me as a so-called *Faculty Innovation Fellow Candidate*. The University Innovation Fellows program focuses on empowering students and, in turn, the two-year faculty program aims to support mentors to achieve this. For me, a substantial part of this project is to develop a solid proposition of what Entrepreneurial Mindfulness is and how it could become a thing.

And this book is my attempt to do just that. During the last few months, I read, I thought, I talked to people, I thought again, I systematically stopped thinking (i.e. I meditated) and, of course, I wrote down my ideas. I want to take you on this journey. I believe that sustainable change requires us to create the future from the present moment and to appreciate the wholeness of ourselves and our connectedness to anything and everything. And I believe that:

**Entrepreneurial Mindfulness empowers changemakers to sustainably create the future from the present moment. It combines an entrepreneurial mindset with the ability to consciously envision a desirable future while mindfully acting in the present moment. A mode that I also refer to as "Being-while-Striving". Furthermore, Entrepreneurial Mindfulness implies having the compassion to appreciate our planetary and our individual boundaries.**

You are in the comfortable situation of being able to venture into this journey with a definition at hand. I did not! It emerged, and it evolved, I refined it and finally turned it into the three sentences above. In the remainder of this book, you will learn how to meet the dark side of entrepreneurial passion with mindfulness and compassion, get to know about all the facets of this definition and understand why I defined it this way.

I bet you are curious now and want to learn more about the ideas behind Entrepreneurial Mindfulness. In order to do that, our next perspective will be a visual one. After all, a picture is worth a thousand words.

## Painting a Picture of Entrepreneurial Mindfulness

Personally, I believe that as entrepreneurs we have great power and responsibility. We are shaping resource flows, developing technologies, spreading new ideas and creating products that will shape the lives of future generations. We also have great responsibility towards ourselves, which we will discuss in more detail later. So, when we talk about entrepreneurship and mindfulness, I suggest we should guide our mindfulness in two directions: being mindful of what the world needs and being mindful of what we need. Indeed, some research goes as far as to investigate how mindfulness practice might connect our *own well-being* with *planetary well-being*.[2] How might we project our ideas into the future while staying aware of and acting in the present moment? I am looking forward to sharing how I explored this apparent paradox. Because the definition of Entrepreneurial Mindfulness I have just proposed is quite complex, I also visualized my idea in the *Entrepreneurial Mindfulness Diagram* in Figure 1 on the next page.

Much more accessible, right? Let me explain this in more detail. Firstly, I was inspired by the *Ikigai Venn Diagram* after reading the book *Ikigai* by Héctor García and Francesc Miralles.[3] By the way, rumor has it that the diagram does not really reflect the original Japanese idea of Ikigai.[4] Either way, I think it is pretty much on point for capturing what many people call *purpose-driven entrepreneurship*, which we will discuss in Chapter 1. To me, it seems reasonable to argue that something you love, you can get paid for, the world needs and you are good at deserves your heart, mind and energy.

My personal purpose is to empower changemakers to drive sustainable change while living happy and fulfilled lives. But I would also like to propose a tiny addition to the framework. As someone who is currently working on his PhD in innovation

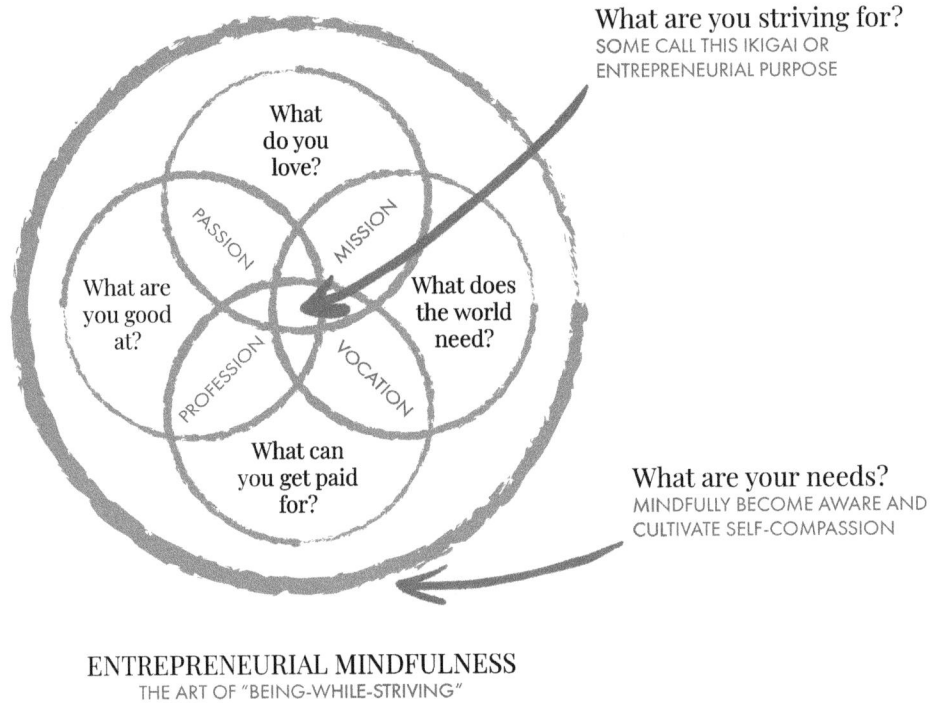

**What are you striving for?**
SOME CALL THIS IKIGAI OR
ENTREPRENEURIAL PURPOSE

What
do you
love?

PASSION

MISSION

What are
you good
at?

What does
the world
need?

PROFESSION

VOCATION

What can
you get paid
for?

**What are your needs?**
MINDFULLY BECOME AWARE AND
CULTIVATE SELF-COMPASSION

**ENTREPRENEURIAL MINDFULNESS**
THE ART OF "BEING-WHILE-STRIVING"

*Figure 1: Entrepreneurial Mindfulness Diagram. Based on García and Miralles (2017).*

management, educating future changemakers and started the process of founding his own venture, I am missing an important aspect. My awareness of the missing part originates from my own movement and mindfulness practice. It is quite simply *you*! Or me. Or anyone else making the effort to create a world that is a little bit better. It's stressful... It's ambiguous... It requires energy and hard work. And there is a limit to what we can *give*.

So I would like to propose an adapted version of this visualization of Ikigai. I suggest that when we go out and change the world, we stay mindful of the present moment and ourselves. That we mindfully become aware of our own needs, appreciate them, and bless us with loads of self-compassion. Of course, there is no reason why your capacity cannot be cultivated, too. If you cannot change something today, it doesn't mean that you cannot change it tomorrow. We become what we repeatedly do and I am happy to support you in finding your practice with the exercises provided at the end of every chapter. However, every human being in every present moment has limitations. To me, the *serenity prayer*, which opened this chapter and is often attributed to Reinhold Niebur, finds the most elegant and timeless words to describe this idea. Respect your limitations. Respect yourself. Be mindful of your own personal capacity. Find the fine line between grit and taking self-responsibility. I believe (and science supports this) that there are severe consequences for not doing that. So, entrepreneurial well-being is one of the perspectives we will need to bear in mind in our journey towards a better understanding of Entrepreneurial Mindfulness in Chapter 2. Let me introduce the remaining perspectives I will share to explore a mindful and compassionate approach to entrepreneurship and why it is an idea worth "making a thing".

## A Roadmap for Exploring Entrepreneurial Mindfulness

In this book, we will be exploring the interplay of entrepreneurship and mindfulness in four parts: a roadmap for how to dig deeper into the hearts and minds of mindful changemakers, so to speak. In the respective chapters, we will take several perspectives on why a more mindful and compassionate approach to entrepreneurship is important, how it might look like and how it might become reality. Furthermore, I have reached out to experts in the field and you will find several *Deep Dives*, based on these conversations. Let me briefly introduce the four parts of this book.

### Part One – A Threefold Challenge

In the first part of this book, we will explore *why* the concept of Entrepreneurial Mindfulness matters in the first place. When we talk about entrepreneurs and purpose-driven entrepreneurs in particular, we need to talk about three challenges they face. Zooming out, we see the economic mess of disruptions like Covid-19. It's not the first disruption we have faced, and it will certainly not be the last. The economy has always relied on dedicated entrepreneurs to mobilize resources and get us back on track. In addition, we are increasingly challenged by environmental and social issues. So, entrepreneurs are exposed to the expectation of making a positive economic as well as social impact and we need them to "get us out of the mess".[5] Zooming in a bit more, we can see that entrepreneurs are being challenged to get a viable business running. Whether they are primarily driven by a social or by a commercial goal, they have to have a working business model. Finally, are you ready to meet the "dark side of entrepreneurial passion"?[6] Getting a business running involves hard work and many things that can potentially go wrong, and entrepreneurs also have to handle their internal challenge during the entrepreneurial journey.[7]

## Part Two – The Entrepreneurial Journey

In order to examine the *dark side of entrepreneurial passion*, we need to understand some important mechanics of acting as an entrepreneur. So, we will get a little bit more "technical" in this part of the book. Entrepreneurship is an evolving research field and it boldly takes on various interconnected aspects of bringing ideas into existence and making an impact In Part One of the book, you will have learned important concepts about economic growth, human welfare and some more practical aspects, such as business model-related decisions. However, we are not yet ready to add mindfulness to the equation. This part will shed light on what it means to "become" an entrepreneur, the role of opportunities and the entrepreneurial journey from an internal viewpoint. We will dig deeper into the cognitive perspective on entrepreneurship, and talk about mindsets, purpose and why you need to take your whole self on the entrepreneurial journey.

## Part Three – Infusing Mindfulness

As you will know by now, entrepreneurs are being challenged to create a positive impact, they need to get a viable business running and they need to stay sane and healthy during their entrepreneurial marathon. In Part Two of the book, we got to understand the entrepreneurial journey, intentions and mindsets in more detail. Furthermore, we saw why it might be a good idea to maintain a strong sense of purpose and contribute to "something bigger" than yourself. In Part Three, I add the concept of mindfulness to this equation. As entrepreneurs, we create the future, which is our common denominator. We dwell on things that do not exist yet, because we are convinced that they should come into existence. We spot an opportunity and decide to act! Mindfulness, however, is essentially about being in the present moment and "non-doing". The important point is that science shows plenty of positive effects of cultivating mindfulness on human functioning as well as well-being. Let's explore this apparent paradox and the potential for resolving it by creating the future from the present moment. The two chapters in this part introduce concepts of mindfulness, its relationship to meditation, exciting scientific findings about their effects and an eight-week Entrepreneurial Mindfulness self-experiment.

I believe that the future can indeed be created from the present moment, that we can cultivate a mode of *Being-while-Striving*. Moreover, I believe that this mode will bear many positive effects for entrepreneurs and consequently for a society that will hugely benefit from their actions.

## Part Four – Entrepreneurial Mindfulness

The last part of the book synthesizes the insights, concepts and experiences of the last three parts and suggests ways to "make Entrepreneurial Mindfulness a thing". We all rely on dedicated entrepreneurs to solve our global challenges. Our future truly depends on them. But we also know that this responsibility can have severe effects on people's health and well-being. There is a dark side to entrepreneurial passion. Recent scientific findings and my own experience show that meditation and mindfulness practice can be an important tool for mitigating these negative effects and can also make entrepreneurs more effective in pursuing their visions. Furthermore, mindfulness can be thought of as *heartfulness*, which reveals *compassion* as an integral element of Entrepreneurial Mindfulness. Yet, if changemakers are to create the future from the present moment using mindfulness, compassion and their whole self, they need support along their entire entrepreneurial journey. So, in this part, I will develop ideas for entrepreneurship training and education, entrepreneurial practice and innovation ecosystems to integrate the idea of Entrepreneurial Mindfulness. All of these chapters include Deep Dives with experts in the field.

Now, let's start with *why*!

# A THREEFOLD CHALLENGE

In this part of the book, we will explore why the concept of Entrepreneurial Mindfulness matters in the first place. When we talk about purpose-driven entrepreneurs in particular, we need to talk about three challenges they face. Zooming out, we see the economic mess of disruptions like Covid-19. It is not the first mess of its kind and it will for sure not be the last one. The economy always relied on entrepreneurs to mobilize resources and get us out of them. Moreover, we are increasingly challenged by environmental and social issues. So, entrepreneurs are exposed to an expectation of making a positive impact and we need them to "get us out of the mess".[1] Zooming in a bit more, we see that entrepreneurs are challenged to get a viable business running. Whether they are primarily driven by a social or by a commercial goal, they have to have a working business model.[2] At least, that is my own humble opinion. Lastly, because getting a viable business running involves hard work and many things that can potentially go wrong, entrepreneurs also have to handle an internal challenge.[3] Let's start with a broad perspective and look at the role of entrepreneurs in society.

## PART 01

"The beginning
is the most important
part of the work."

PLATO

# 01 Why Purpose-Driven Entrepreneurship Matters

OK, let's get started. Having looked at the Entrepreneurial Mindfulness Diagram, you will find purpose-driven entrepreneurship at the core of everything. Why does purpose-driven entrepreneurship matter and why do I think that everyone can make a difference? The question "what does the world need?" is at the core of my personal motivation and drive to do the things I do. Besides my very personal worldview, I simply think it matters to our future that we don't stop asking this question. There is so much we can do, and need to do better! The good news is that I also believe that it has never been so easy to implement the kinds of change we want to see.

Let me share my perspective and provide you with some hands-on steps with which to begin your journey to developing business ideas that are driven by a social or sustainable purpose.

## The Role of the Entrepreneur

First of all, entrepreneurs matter — we can trace this thought back to classic economic theory. In Joseph Schumpeter's seminal works on the role of entrepreneurship and innovation for the economy, he famously said that creative destruction is at the core of capitalism. In his view, capitalism is best described as a process of wealth creation and change. Now, there are certainly things that one might be critical about when it comes to capitalism. Nevertheless, it's the system that currently runs this world and, as a mindful entrepreneur, I try to work with "what is" rather than "what I would like it to be". Which doesn't mean that can't we strive to change it, of course!

Anyway, innovation, which brings new ideas into existence for the sake of economic growth, is at the heart of this process. In one of Schumpeter's most influential books *Business Cycles*, he argues that:

**"For actions which consist in carrying out innovations, we reserve the term Enterprise; the individuals who carry them out we call Entrepreneurs."[4]**

Entrepreneurship is a thriving research field and there is a plethora of definitions out there. For now, we will keep it simple and work with this classic, straightforward one. Don't worry, we will get more technical in Part Two. According to Schumpeter, entrepreneurs are those individuals who are responsible for long-term economic growth. I don't want to get lost in theoretical discussions about economics. However, I hope we can agree on the importance of new ventures and the courageous people who drive them. Prominent examples of this dynamic can be found with a quick look at the recent development of companies such as Google, Amazon, Airbnb, Uber... you get the point, right? Many of these fast growing companies did not exist 20, 10 or even 5 years ago and today, they are among the biggest players in their fields. Even more impressive, they often lead industries which they actually created.

However, entrepreneurship is not all about these big ventures. Every country relies on small- and medium-sized businesses to keep the economy running and maintain a lively flow of innovation.

For example, global consulting agency Ernst & Young acknowledged the role of Entrepreneurs in their 2015 Megatrend Report.[5] One of the six identified megatrends is "Entrepreneurship Rising"; they conclude that the growth of many economies will continue to depend on entrepreneurial activity. Nevertheless, something which Mr. Schumpeter might not have anticipated when *Business Cycles* was published in 1939 and which Ernst & Young does not specifically mention in their entrepreneurship megatrend are the limits to economic growth and the severe consequences that come along with it. I believe that the role of the entrepreneur is more important than ever, not only for the economy, but also for societal welfare. Our generation is confronted with challenges like climate change, loss of biodiversity on a global scale, health issues caused by modern lifestyles, social as well as racial inequalities, and more besides. Do you want to make a positive impact? Just pick one of the challenges just mentioned. Let's take a closer look at the United Nations' perspective on that matter.

## Our Global Challenges

In 2015, the members of the United Nations adopted the "17 Sustainable Development Goals".[6] It is a comprehensive set of targets, which represents a call for action to all of us. Have a glance at the goals in Figure 2. According to the UN, they are intended to promote prosperity while caring for our planetary ecosystem until 2030. The goals recognize that the drive to end poverty must be accompanied by strategies that drive the growth of the economy and address social needs at the same time. So they neatly resemble the dual role of entrepreneurs in our society. Methods of promoting education, well-being and social protection ultimately need to tackle climate change and environmental protection for a sustainable future. Describing all of them in detail would be beyond the scope of this chapter, and a lot of the information is publicly available. However, I would like to focus on goal number 8, "Decent Work and Economic Growth" in some more detail, just to provide an example and make the goals a little less abstract. The 2020 SDG report further describes this goal as an endeavor to stimulate sustainable and inclusive economic growth as well as full employment and decent work for all members of our global society. Its ten sub-goals cover aspects such as gender equality in payment, stimulating entrepreneurship and promoting sustainable production. I certainly hope to make a meaningful contribution to that with this book! Since the ongoing pandemic represents a serious threat to these sub-goals and its key performance indicators, such as GDP or employment rates, I believe that supporting entrepreneurship is currently more important than ever.

From my point of view, a shared vision facilitates collaboration by creating direction and legitimacy. So I hope that the goals get traction and support from everyone who can afford to promote them. In my academic profession, I am engaging most specifically in goals 4 and 9: I am doing my best to empower entrepreneurs and promote a higher focus on their well-being, which hopefully also supports goal number 3 and 8. However, based on my work experience at The Institute for Technology and Innovation Management at Hamburg University of Technology and my mission of empowering changemakers, I can say that our society does not only produce new challenges. The *means* of tackling these challenges also become more accessible, which might transform them into opportunities.

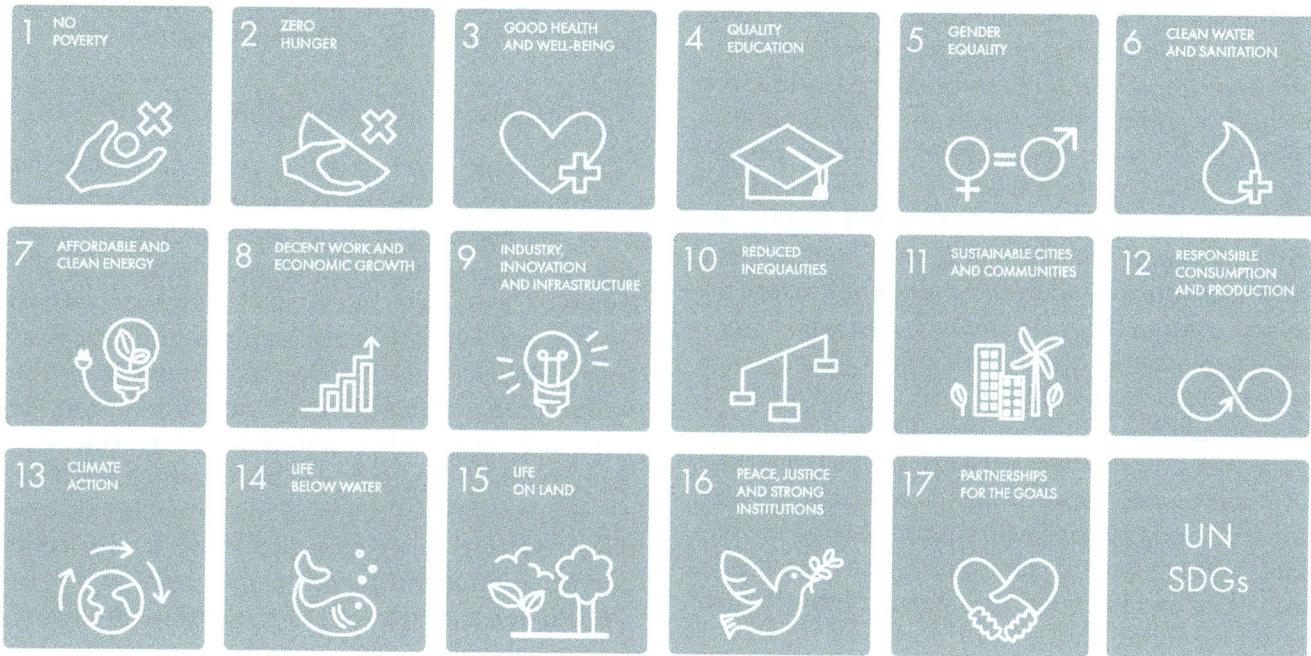

*Figure 2: The United Nations' 17 Sustainable Development Goals (illustrated by Anna-Lena Krohn).*

## Democratizing Innovation and Entrepreneurship

In the 1990s, Professor Eric von Hippel started to challenge the prevailing paradigm that innovation always happens in big corporate research labs. Instead, he suggested that in history the users themselves often came up with solutions and that the means for doing so were increasingly available to the public. This links to the notion of "democratizing innovation".[7] Later on, the idea of user innovation was transformed into a formalized innovation method in collaboration with my PhD supervisor Professor Cornelius Herstatt from Hamburg University of Technology.[8] In this method, organizations systematically look out for so-called *lead users* and collaborate with them in innovation processes. Lead users are individuals who have needs that are not yet catered for by the market, and who have a serious interest in coming up with solutions themselves. Popular examples of user innovated products include the mountain bike, kite surfing equipment and many software solutions, which are often distributed under open source licenses. In his latest book, Eric von Hippel even speaks of "free Innovation".[9] Whatever you want to call it, I agree that the craft of innovation is increasingly available to all of us. Let me share why.

The level of access to knowledge and technology today makes it ever more feasible to actually take the ideas from your mind into existence. You can collaboratively brainstorm and develop ideas in distributed teams using tools like Miro, find important information through search engines, access it in open knowledge sharing platforms, acquire missing skills through open education initiatives, find a local "makerspace" to build a prototype and raise your funds on crowd-funding platforms. Of course, varying levels of access to money, the internet and other resources are creating inequalities, but I would still argue that innovating has never been so accessible for so many people. I designed and launched my website within ten days for about 100 Euros. Of course, this is only the first of many steps towards a successful venture, but I was quickly able to share my message and test if there was a need for it. It was one of my first personal steps towards becoming a purpose-driven entrepreneur.

## The Purpose-Driven Entrepreneur

Now, I would like to have a closer look at some examples of successful purpose-driven entrepreneurs. By the way, you will often find the term social or sustainable entrepreneurship used in this context.[10] However, in the next chapters, we will look at the internal processes and challenges of entrepreneurs. Therefore, the term *purpose-driven* seems more suitable to me. It rather relates to the internal drive for action than describing an external impact, which hopefully will be the result. Anyway, it's easy to look at the obvious examples of creative destroyers, like Elon Musk. He is very clear and open about his purpose when he says that he created Tesla to accelerate a sustainable future.[11] But we can't all become Elon Musks, right? And we don't have to!

There are other inspiring examples. One of my all-time favorites is David Hakkens and his venture Precious Plastic, which is a global community of individuals engaged in tackling the plastic waste problem. Fundamentally, it empowers individuals all over the world with open source technology to recycle plastic, providing a marketplace for machines and raw materials as well as products and a community platform. The coolest thing about it? It all started as a university design project by one single student in 2012.[12]

Not the global community starting kind of person? Fair enough. Let's talk about my friend and personal hero Susanne! She is a certified *design thinking* coach and wholehearted human being. Because she is so smart, she decided to innovate the way we *think*. Instead of linear "take-make-waste" models, she wants to see a more circular type of innovation (cf. SDG goal number 12). So, she integrates the well-refined design thinking framework with circular economy-based approaches into her *circular thinking* framework.[13] She is working with German multinationals, SMEs and NGOs to create the world she wants to live in. As you can see, there are many ways the SDGs can be interpreted and turned into opportunities. We all have gifts that can make an important difference.

Which goal resonates with you? What can you do with your unique set of skills and talents? Where do you want to see your light shine? If you want to commit to what I call purpose-driven entrepreneurship, these questions are probably a good place to start. Bear your answers in mind or write them down on a sticky note (really, there's no innovation without sticky notes) for the exercise at the end of this chapter!

Let's have a glance on what else you need to consider In this chapter, we had a closer look at the "what the world needs" part of purpose-driven entrepreneurship. Creating the world we want to see is a huge motivation. But don't stop there. Other aspects are important to consider, if you truly want to bring about sustainable change. You will face difficulties and you will go through periods of having no clue what you are doing (if you encounter the beautiful world of German taxes, for example). This is a natural part of doing something that potentially hasn't been done before (a.k.a. innovation). Are you clear about your abilities? Your passions? Oh... and who will pay your rent, by the way? We will talk about the transition from motivation to starting a venture to actually bringing it into existence in Part Two. Feel free to jump back to the Entrepreneurial Mindfulness Diagram in the introduction for a visual guide. I believe the Ikigai Venn Diagram is a fantastic way to capture the aspects that will get you through this. So what is holding many of us back from making an impact? Besides resource inequalities, I believe there are also inequalities regarding the extend to which we believe in ourselves. Sadly, this is also backed by science.

## What is Holding You Back?

In my PhD research about mindsets, I came across Carol Dweck's work on *growth* and *fixed mindsets*.[14] Her theory provides a great example of how our self-beliefs and the language we use about ourselves shapes our behavior and its outcome. In more general terms, she differentiates between two groups of people. When confronted with a challenge, the first group of people approaches it with an attitude of curiosity and sees an opportunity to learn and grow. They believe that their abilities can develop through challenging situations so they have what Carol Dweck defines as a *growth mindset*. By contrast, the second group of people sees challenging situations as a moment of judgement. You pass a test? You're good enough. You fail? You're not. In their *fixed mindset*, intelligence is something that you are either born with or not.

A very powerful word that distinguishes the one from the other is *yet*! Maybe you can't do something right now, but that doesn't mean you cannot learn it. So you can't do it, yet. How do you approach life? Next time you're facing a challenge, observe how you react if things don't turn out like you expected. Ultimately, the word yet creates a path into the future. It is a path of mindfully cultivating your personal capacity to do epic stuff!

Interestingly, our upbringing has a lot to do with the way we see ourselves. In one study, Dweck told a group of students that that every time they get out of their comfort zone to learn something new, the neurons in their brains can form new connections and over time they can get smarter. The other group did not receive this "growth mindset treatment". Guess what? The growth mindset group showed significant improvements in math performance after the treatment, which has been replicated in other studies and even published in the famous journal *Nature*.[15] Sadly, according to Carol Dweck, there are great mindset inequalities inherent in culture, ethnicity and socio-economic status.

So, how did you grow up? How did your parents, teachers and friends talk to you? From the bottom of my heart, I kindly ask you to let go of all the shit that doesn't serve you. You define your value, you decide where you want to go and you decide who you want to become. You will still have to do the work, but science has got your back!

## In a Nutshell...

I don't mind whether you want to talk about social, sustainable, or purpose-driven entrepreneurs. I believe that we need them all. We need all the ideas we can find to tackle the economic, environmental and social challenges of our global society. Making a positive impact is the first of the threefold challenges that entrepreneurs are entangled in. The good news is that it has become more and more feasible for many of us to make an impact through innovation and entrepreneurship. Crucial knowledge is shared openly, and technology is getting more accessible and affordable.

However, be aware that starting this journey eventually begins within you. Whether you decide that the constant change and ambiguity of a dynamic global society is a threat or an opportunity, lies within your very own perception. I don't mean to say that becoming an entrepreneur doesn't come at a certain price. Joseph Schumpeter puts it this way:

**"Times of innovation are times of effort and sacrifice, of work for the future, while the harvest comes after."** [16]

We will look at the challenges and potential sacrifices of entrepreneurs in the next chapter. However, something in this chapter is still missing. Right, you! Start honing your entrepreneurial mindset right now! In this exercise, I want you to dwell on a future that you would like to see and practice your own creative confidence.

# I Dare You:

## Create Your Entrepreneurial Vision!

- Take some time for yourself, go for a walk, take a bath or do anything that helps you to get some headspace
- Reflect on the 17 goals
  - Which goals resonate with you?
  - Which goals matter most to you?
- Do your homework
  - What are the specific SDG sub-goals?
  - What are relevant new technologies, trends and social developments?
- How might you turn this combination into an opportunity and make an impact?
- Reflect on your strengths and crucial skills that you maybe did not learn (yet)
- Challenge your self-beliefs
  - What is holding you back?
  - Ask some people who matter to you, if they would confirm these limiting beliefs
- Reflect on the things that you love doing
- Make a mental list of things that are absolutely crucial for your well-being
  - Right, you are encouraged to be mindful of your own needs!
- Be realistic about your budget and how much you can work on this in the coming weeks and months
- Grab some paper or sticky notes and take the first step
  - Brainstorm a name for your venture
  - Scribble a logo
  - Train your creative muscle
- Talk to someone and get your idea out into the world!

„Courage is
resistance to fear,
mastery of fear,
not absence of fear."

MARK TWAIN

# 02 All That Glitters Is Not Gold

Don't get me wrong, I do believe that purpose-driven entrepreneurs are incredibly important for our global society. Living your dream, being your own boss and striving for a future you want to live in can be fulfilling and rewarding. I hope that I made that point in the last chapter. However, there are aspects of the process that are less glamorous and I want to have an honest conversation about them. In this chapter, we will look at entrepreneurial well-being and the challenges of staying mindful in times of stress, change and uncertainty.

This chapter is also the first one to conclude with a Deep Dive section. The researcher in me does not trust my own opinion very much. So, I challenge my ideas with experts in the field. This chapter's Deep Dive is a conversation with Rogelio Arellano. Roger is the co-founder as well as CTO at Citruslabs and a two times "Forbes 30 under 30 Social Entrepreneurs" alumnus. Hence, he might have some things to share about the entrepreneurial journey. Also, he is an entirely wholehearted human being and I am happy to call him my friend! Before we get to the conversation, I would like to set the stage with my own initial thoughts, important concepts and research findings.

## Startups and Failure

Let's recall from the introduction that startups aim to develop new services or products under *conditions of extreme uncertainty*. No pressure but... A commonly cited number for new product failures is 80%.[17] However, empirical research from high quality innovation, marketing and product development journals suggests failure rates around 40% instead.[18] I don't want to go into too much detail about the higher figure, which has even been called an "urban legend", but George Castellion and Stephen Markham have collected some pretty intriguing arguments that the self-interest of consultants or successful product managers might play a role here.[19] According to them, those who are engaged in developing successful new products might want to see their lights shine even brighter and professional service providers might want to convince their customers of their necessity. Anyway, the point either way is that bringing new ideas to life is a risky and complex venture. Whether it is 2 out of 5 or 4 out of 5 ideas that never make it into a viable business, you want to make damn sure your idea isn't one of them! Today, "fail faster" is a motto that you hear a lot in the startup world. I generally agree with that philosophy and Eric Ries made a pretty good point in his book *The Lean Startup*.[20] Basically, he suggests that you are well advised to continuously assess your venture in a "build, measure, learn" cycle. If you are new to the world of entrepreneurship, this is one of my number one recommended books to read. It is easy to grasp and provides a good foundation in the basics of bringing your ideas into existence.

Gone are the days of business plans in which you pretend to actually know what's going on. Which doesn't mean you should not think things through thoroughly, of course... It simply means that building a startup is not something you do in your head but in the world out there. So, you should challenge your own ideas as early as possible. For example, you might consider the conversation at the end of this chapter an early user test. After all, product-related assumptions might be wrong, and a realistic consequence would be product failure. Surely you want to prevent that by all means. At that stage, you have probably already decided to make personal sacrifices, not started a decently-paid job or made similar trade-offs. Chances are that you are "all-in". So, what do you do? Sure, you work your ass off! Who wouldn't? And we weren't even talking specifically within the context of purpose-driven entrepreneurs. You found a cause that gets you up in the morning, because it kept you from sleeping in peace in the first place? What do you do? You work even harder!

Are you starting to get the idea of me drawing a circle around the entire purpose-driven entrepreneurship side of things in the Entrepreneurial Mindfulness Diagram? Constantly being engaged in thinking about the future and, potentially, worrying about it, might not quite merge with mindfully creating the future from the present moment. Of course, we always have expectations about how we want things to turn out, but things might well turn out differently. Getting a viable business running is a complex, challenging task. Let's have a look at a tool that supports entrepreneurs to grasp and reduce this complexity into a set of more manageable tasks.

## The Challenge of a Viable Business Model

Let's have a look at my adaptation of the *business model canvas in Figure 3*. This tool was originally developed by Alexander Osterwalder, building on the insights of his PhD project.[21] It summarizes all the important things you have to think of when starting a new venture or adapting an existing business model. Bear in mind that you will not only have to think about them, but plan to turn them into reality, and actually test and execute them. However, the business model canvas is a powerful tool for breaking down and grasping this complexity. I admire Alexander Osterwalder for turning solid academic work into something that is so accessible. Let's have a closer look at the tool itself.

Whether you are familiar with the business model canvas tool or not, you can immediately see that there is quite a lot of stuff going on. Usually, when people think about starting their own business, they do so with a core idea about *what* they want to share with the world. This could be a product, a service or a digital experience. Most importantly, it is something that should provide some kind of value to somebody. While this is the best case scenario, it requires rigorous testing and an openness to potential customers not placing the value on your product that you thought they would. Alexander Osterwalder and his team have dedicated an entire book to testing business ideas.[22] In Chapter 9, we will take a closer look at design thinking, which is a great approach to systemizing this process and crafting solid value propositions.

For my mission, I decided to adapt the canvas slightly and add a "Your Purpose" building block — just to make sure you stay connected to the reason that got you here in the first place. Feel free to take the canvas as a follow-up to the exercise from the last chapter. Once you are clear about your reason for starting the entrepreneurial journey and you are confident that your *value proposition* is rock solid, you need to think about the ways you

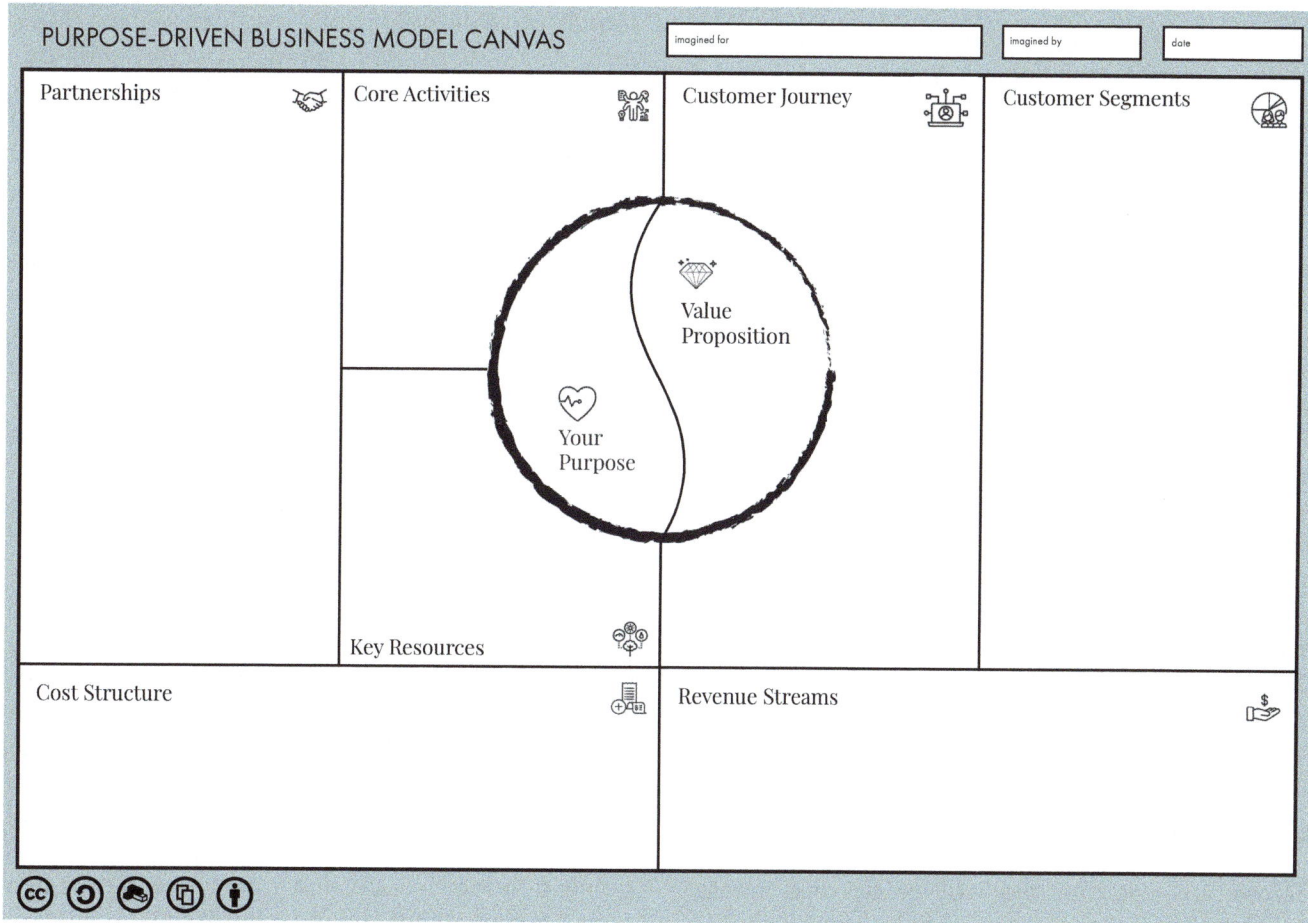

**PURPOSE-DRIVEN BUSINESS MODEL CANVAS**

imagined for | imagined by | date

Partnerships

Core Activities

Customer Journey

Customer Segments

Value Proposition

Your Purpose

Key Resources

Cost Structure

Revenue Streams

*Figure 3: The purpose-driven business model canvas is a derivate of the business model canvas by Strategyzer AG (2021). Used under CC BY-SA 3.0.*

create value. This entails thinking about important *partnerships*, *core activities* and *key resources*. Depending on the nature of your product, service or experience, this can of course vary quite substantially. Furthermore, you will have to deliver your value to your *customer segments* via well-crafted *customer journeys*. Finally, you have to make ends meet and think about capturing value.

Your *cost structure* and *revenue streams* obviously need to allow for a *viable* business model. So, there are many things to take care of and I could probably write an entire book just about business models. Luckily, Alexander Osterwalder already did that for us![23] What's most important for our understanding is that you basically have to do all this by yourself or in a small team. Moreover, more often than not, you will be doing it from scratch. Ultimately, this gives you the edge and a competitive advantage over big, slow-moving organizations. However, it is a big challenge, as we will learn in our Deep Dive with Rogelio later in this chapter. But how might this external business challenge translate into the inner world of entrepreneurs? How might this situation of ambiguity and the stressful pressure to fight various battles at once affect the mental and physical health of changemakers?

## A Glance at the Continuum of Well-Being and Mental Health

Before we consider the well-being and mental health of entrepreneurs, we should have a shared understanding of the idea of well-being and mental health. The World Health Organization, which is arguably one of the most central global institutions when it comes to health, states in its constitution that health is not just the absence of illness. It is also de-fined by a condition of "complete physical, mental and social well-being".[24]

In that sense, well-being is a complex construct. Moreover, it is inherently connected to health, which includes mental health, of course. Respectively, research on well-being takes various perspectives, such as physical well-being, economic well-being, social well-being, emotional well-being or mental well-being. The Centers for Disease Control and Prevention (CDC), a division of the U.S. Department of Health and Human Services, provides a publicly available, rich overview of well-being concepts, including definitions and measurement scales.[25] For our discussion, we will work with the CDC's suggestion that well-being is meaningful for many sectors of society and the humans interacting in them. In simple terms, it provides a concept for understanding whether people perceive their lives as worth living. This subjective dimension is important, because merely considering living conditions, such as housing and employment, is not sufficient for defining how people actually *perceive* their situation. While objective measures are fundamental to well-being, indicators that measure how people feel and think about their lives are key to developing a holistic picture. I suppose everyone can relate to that idea. Objectively, everything might be going perfectly, but a big fight with our partner or a relative being sick can totally occupy our individual perception of how things are going. Thus, the ongoing academic discussion addresses experience of positive emotions (*hedonic* tradition), realization of individual human potential (*eudaimonic* tradition) or overall life satisfaction. Basically, looking at a person's living situation from the outside and "hard facts", like salary data doesn't give you any clue about how that person feels about her or his life. How supportive and healthy are their important relationships? How do they react to the pressure of performing in a well-paid but challenging job? Does that job actually provide any meaning and fulfillment? These are fundamental questions when it comes to *happy* and *fulfilled* lives, which are also discussed in seminal works, such as Victor Frankl's *Man's Search For Meaning*.[26] Lastly, Ute Stephan suggests that well-being and mental health may be understood as a continuum.[27] One end of the continuum represents a state of full psychological functioning and happiness. The other end can be characterized by *mental ill-being*, such as burnout, personality disorders or depression.

Let's have a look at one of the most widely applied scales for measuring subjective psychological well-being, the "WHO-5 Well-Being Index".[28] While only covering five questions and thus being comparatively short, it is successfully applied by scholars as a generic scale for well-being across many study fields. For the scale, study participants indicate whether the following statements applied at *no time*, *some of the time*, *less than half the time*, *more than half the time*, *most of the time* or *all of the time* during the last two weeks:

- I have felt cheerful and in good spirits
- I have felt calm and relaxed
- I have felt active and vigorous
- I woke up feeling fresh and rested
- My daily life has been filled with things that interest me

What I like about the scale is that it is easy to grasp how this relates to everyday challenges, like being stressed, being "in your head" too much, not being able to sleep at night or constantly dealing with unfulfilling tasks. Also, it shows that subjective well-being is really about how you internally relate to the things that are going on in your life. This will be a crucial thing to bear in mind when we discuss the mindfulness-related aspects of our journey in more detail. When we look back at the situation of entrepreneurs, we can find factors that might promote their well-being and ones that might be more challenging. On the one hand, ideally, entrepreneurs are highly autonomous, choose the idea they are working on and might experience more motivation by filling their working days with interesting tasks. On the other hand, they often work on their own and are usually emotionally connected to their ideas. This is why entrepreneurial fear of failure is a hot topic in entrepreneurship research[29] — we will revisit this topic in a later chapter.

It is easy to get bogged in hypothetical monologues on this subject, which is not the purpose of this book. So let's look at some empirical research and then talk to an actual entrepreneur to hear some real life experiences.

## On Entrepreneurial Well-Being and Mental Health

My interest in this topic was sparked by various conversations with changemakers who seemed tired and stressed, and who did not seem to take much part in life outside of their own ventures anymore. I have a strong passion for innovation and entrepreneurship, and I believe that driving change is crucial for our future. However, I still think that there is more to life and I always advocate a healthy balance in every aspect of life. To me, it seems that this balance often gets lost when it comes to changemakers who are really passionate about their work.

Overall, research on entrepreneurial well-being acknowledges the idea that starting a venture can be a highly stressful, long and tedious journey and contrasts this with meaningful, satisfying tasks. Accordingly, Johan Wiklund and his colleagues discuss entrepreneurial well-being as a multifaceted phenomenon.[30] Their conceptualization entails all the well-being aspects that entrepreneurs experience in the endeavor of creating and running a startup. While interest in the domain of entrepreneurial well-being is quickly growing, many questions remain open and research is rather fragmented across disciplines.[31] For the purpose of this chapter, we will look at a recent empirical study, which particularly highlights "the dark side" of entrepreneurs' well-being and mental health. By the way, even The World Economic Forum is keeping a close eye on a potential mental health crisis among entrepreneurs. Their interest in the topic got sparked by the following study.[32] Michael Freeman from the University of California in San Francisco, along with several other researchers published a study in 2018, which surveyed 242 entrepreneurs and 93 comparison participants in the US.[33] The researchers' main hypothesis is that the prevalence of depression, substance use disorders and other mental health issues among entrepreneurs is higher than among other people.

Sadly, their sample revealed that entrepreneurs report a lifetime history with twice as many cases of depression, a six-fold greater prevalence of ADHD, a three-fold greater prevalence of substance use disorders and an eleven-fold greater prevalence of bipolar disorder. Both groups reported similar levels of anxiety. Furthermore, 49% of entrepreneurs in the study report having one mental health condition during their lives. 32% report having two or more mental health conditions and 18% report having three or more mental health conditions. Nevertheless, the study does not investigate causal relationships between entrepreneurial activities and mental health conditions. Personal predispositions of entrepreneurs might also play an important role. In any case, mental health awareness is a very important topic for entrepreneurs! I personally believe there is a "dark side of entrepreneurial passion" and another study revealed that obsessively passionate entrepreneurs are facing a higher risk of suffering from burnout.[34] Other studies might show different results and, as we have noted, there are many upsides to becoming an entrepreneur. For example, Nadav Shir and Carol Ryff recently published a comprehensive conceptual framework of aspects of the entrepreneurial journey that promote eudaimonic well-being, as we will see in the next part of the book.[35] In particular, they suggest that a sense of *purpose, autonomy, positive relations, environmental mastery, personal growth* and *self-acceptance* are factors that can be harnessed by individuals who pursue the creation of a business venture. I believe that these aspects could buffer the negative effects, and the *perceived well-being* of entrepreneurs might be comparable to that of non-entrepreneurs. Furthermore, Shir and Ryff suggest we should fundamentally rethink how we assess the *success* of entrepreneurial ventures, going beyond the economic impact and taking into account their self-fulfilling and society-serving potentials.

I certainly agree that the entrepreneurial journey can be highly fulfilling. It could even be deemed to be a deeply spiritual experience of self-actualization. Nevertheless, I think that the dark side of entrepreneurial well-being and mental health should be taken very seriously. We need to destigmatize mental health and there should be absolutely no shame in seeking professional help. I also believe that there are better ways of preparing people for the entrepreneurial journey, which is of course the whole point of this book. We will discuss in more detail what might happen if we add mindfulness to the equation in Part Three. At this point, I feel like the stage is ready for Rogelio and some first-hand insights from his experiences. And don't worry; he will also share some inspiring and uplifting thoughts!

# Deep Dive

## A Conversation with Rogelio Arellano,
## the Humble Entrepreneur

Malte: Hey Roger, it is so good to see you! So, you are co-founder and CTO at Citruslabs, formerly Mindmate, and you made it into the "Forbes 30 under 30 Social Entrepreneurs" twice. Quite impressive, I would say! I would love to learn more about your experiences of going through the startup journey, challenges that you faced and strategies for dealing with all that. Since we are friends, I already know the "hard facts" of your story, but would you share in a few sentences how you got started for the people who don't know you, yet?

Roger: Sure, I will! So after I graduated in Mexico, I always wanted to go to Europe and pursue a master's degree. I got into the Global Innovation Management program at the University of Strathclyde in Glasgow, UK. Also, I always had on my mind to have my own business when I came here. Then, during the program, I had all these cool courses about product design, startups, marketing and everything to get this started. Eventually, I also ended up in two startup competitions. They were more than inspiring and I was meeting all these people that help you in developing your ideas and connect you with people who have the right skills and knowledge. In the first one, I got into the finals and in the second one, I met my co-founder. We developed the idea for Mindmate and we won! At the beginning, Mindmate was only a rough idea for supporting families with people that suffered from dementia using technology. We decided to take things forward from there. So that was basically the beginning. Now, Mindmate is Citruslabs, we have 15 employees and obviously a lot of things happened.

Malte: Well, sometimes things happen so quickly, right? And you kept on working on that idea, and got into several accelerator programs. In 2016 you even went through the Techstars accelerator program in New York. As I told you beforehand, I want to explore the reasons why well-being is such a challenge for many entrepreneurs. I guess, going through this process was not always easy. What were your biggest challenges in taking care of your physical, mental and social well-being?

Roger: At the very beginning, I was super excited about this. In my mind, this thing would pick up super quickly and we would make millions in a matter of two years. Maybe I have just read too many of these success stories! Well, that was my idea. But I think that it is really important to understand, especially for starting entrepreneurs, that you are in for a long, slow ride. So, it is really important to stay in balance from the very beginning. It is not a fast race that you need to make. You are rather running a marathon than a sprint. You need to have a balance in your pace. If you go too fast, you will burn out and miss so many important aspects of your life, like friends, your social circle or maybe your family. If you only focus on one thing, you will burn out. Better to prepare for a marathon. In my case, I was so excited at the beginning that I was fully committed to my idea. I would spend nights working on designs and the app. The whole team was working a lot, too. We were working on the tech and the business model with just three people. There is a lot of pressure from there as well. Your team is giving 100%. Of course, you are also giving 100%! You need to be in the same mental state as them. Things were getting a bit more complicated when we had gotten investment from an accelerator during the summer of 2015. There was a lot of work to do, I still had to finish my master's and my brother got married. I ended up not going to my brother's wedding, which is something I regret to this day.

Malte: As we lived together, I remember your insanely long working nights and you even defending your thesis from a coffee shop in New York, if I remember correctly. Anyway, is this something you would do differently today?

Roger: Definitely! I was putting a lot of focus on the company and everything else was secondary. I think that is something I wouldn't do anymore. Just taking a couple of days off will usually not screw your venture. Today, I would put my family first, refresh and go back and give my 100%. However, back then I was so committed because the venture was also my ticket to stay in Europe. I needed to make this work after all the energy I put in.

Malte: I sense there is something like personal sunk costs going on. If you turn around at some point, you feel like all the effort was for nothing?

Roger: Yes, exactly! But to be honest, I don't feel that way anymore. Now, I think that everything I have experienced and learned was so great. It is certainly not lost, even if we couldn't take the company forward from here. I am very grateful for that experience.

Malte: That is so interesting. I would like to pick up on that. So when you are getting started with all that, you are probably really attached to that one idea or business and nowadays you see the things that you learned and your network. Do you get more relaxed about the whole topic of failure?

Roger: Yes, because you learn a lot of things and one of them is that a lot of startups will fail. Many ideas fail and probably your first idea will. It is a learning process and, at the beginning, it was all about that one idea. Today, I am more open to the possibility that it will be an idea that comes further down the line. I am not scared of starting something new at some point anymore. The fear of failing is gone. Many people will have this fear when they start, but failing is OK. It is really about picking yourself up and trying something new. At the beginning, you don't have that.

Malte: You say that entrepreneurship is more of a marathon than a sprint. I love that metaphor. When you really set your mind on something and want to go forward, there is no way to avoid getting out of your comfort zone. Making sacrifices and working hard is probably inevitable if you want to take part in shaping the future. But how do you know if it is a bit too much and you are risking burnout, depression or other negative effects? Do you have some advice for finding that fine line between grit and not appreciating your personal capacity?

Roger: As you said, it is a fine line. At the very beginning, we really needed to put in our 100%, but you have to be aware of this problem. If you have a deadline and it has to happen, do it! Set up a schedule for the important week, but be aware of your needs and give yourself time off. Saturday, Sunday or an important event with friends. There should always be time for this. I think it is all about self-awareness. There are times where the company will need your 100%. Still, you should balance this. In my case, there were times with a lot of pressure and deadlines and without me noticing, I stopped eating properly. I would wake up, connect with the team and at 2 or 3 pm I would realize that I had not eaten anything. Then I would grab an apple or a coffee and work for another four hours. At this point, you can't be productive anymore and you are sacrificing your health. Just taking time for eating stressed me out. Then, I was getting sick, which made everything worse, because you need to recover. It is more sustainable to take your time, take a walk, eat properly and then do what you have to do. Another thing that I did was to neglect my friends and family. This is also not good. It's all about self-awareness really. This is something that you want to learn right from the beginning. In order to be prepared for that marathon you need to take care of your personal mental and physical well-being, your friends and family and keep your vision in mind. You really have to be driven by some kind of purpose!

Malte: That was so inspiring Roger! I am curious now. So you say that things like self-awareness, time management and taking care of your well-being are crucial. Is that something that entrepreneurs learn in university education or accelerators or is it something that needs more attention?

Roger: Definitely, it should receive more attention! I don't remember having a seminar about these kinds of topics at all. It was never brought up in my training. Instead, it was something that I looked up when I was feeling a little bit down or stressed out. Then, I was finding stories about other entrepreneurs who were totally going through what I was experiencing. I don't think this is brought up enough, and I think it is really important to bring this into workshops for starting entrepreneurs. Because when you know that this is something you might be going through, then you can start looking out for these cues and develop strategies for coping with them.

Malte: Well, I agree and feel that mindfulness might be just the right tool for entrepreneurs. What pops up in your mind when you hear the term Entrepreneurial Mindfulness?

Roger: Well, I think it is very important to maintain very good mental well-being. It is absolutely vital if you want to put a lot of passion into something that you want to work on. Also, being connected with your environment and the people around you is very important for that. Ultimately, by being connected to people, you are more aware of the things that can make a difference in the world. That's how I see it. Also, there will be ups and downs and you will need a social web to support you. At the end of the day, you are here for a limited amount of time. You want to make a difference, yes! But you also want to live a happy and fulfilled life. You need tools and strategies for that. In my case, hiking is a good tool. I also started meditating and using breathing techniques. Today, I'm really doing well, but I learned a lot even in the last year. For example, letting go of the fear of failing.

Malte: Roger, I am so happy that you took your time to share your experiences, struggles and strategies for dealing with that. Hopefully, we can support changemakers to navigate these challenges more smoothly.

## In a Nutshell...

In this chapter, we introduced two more challenges that entrepreneurs are confronted with. First, they need to get a viable business running, which is a challenging task in its own right. Creating, delivering and capturing value with your business model requires creativity, iterations and hard work. To put in Rogelio's beautiful words, better prepare for a marathon than for a sprint. Looking at current scientific work, we can see that this external entrepreneurial challenge also implies an internal one. Possibly, this internal challenge can have severe effects on the mental health and well-being of entrepreneurs. Building on Rogelio's personal experience and recent studies, I challenge you to consciously and thoroughly prepare to:

- Take care of your mental health and don't hesitate to seek professional help
- Develop strategies to cope with emotional challenges, like the fear of failure
- Take care of your physical well-being
- Nourish meaningful social connections
- Stay connected to your purpose (we will revisit this in Part Two)

While sometimes you might have to push your boundaries in one of these aspects (e.g. skip a night out with your friends), you should maintain an overall balance in life and find ways to deal with the stress of starting and running a business. In that sense, this would be a good point to revisit the definition of Entrepreneurial Mindfulness. I hope in this chapter, Rogelio and I were able to make the point that being mindful about one's own capacity is important and that entrepreneurs need to develop strategies to mindfully cultivate this capacity in the long run. Indeed, Jon-Kabat Zinn (who will be thoroughly introduced in Chapter 5) suggests that we might develop a lack of awareness of the web of life that surrounds us by constantly compromising our present moment in favor of moments to come in the future.[36]

I believe that current entrepreneurship education, training and practice is not where it could be in this regard. So, I want to directly put these insights into action and share a simple exercise with you right now. Entrepreneurship is about creating the future and, yes, you will need to plan, work hard and sacrifice more immediate pleasures in exchange for more fulfilling outcomes in the future. However, it is imperative for your well-being to understand the fine line between anticipating what might come and trying to control things that you cannot control! The next time your thoughts get caught in the latter kind of pattern, try the following exercise. These kinds of exercises require practice and dedication, which is why we talk about cultivation. There will be much more about this in Part Three and Four. You will need a conscious commitment as well as continuous practice to feel the changes. Ultimately, they should help you to direct your energy to where it needs to go and improve your overall well-being.

# I Dare You:

## Create the Future From the Present Moment!

- Take a short break from whatever you are doing
- Wrap your mind around the situation or the aspect of it that stresses you or makes you feel uncomfortable
- Try to clearly distinguish between facets that you can directly influence and things that are not under your control (e.g. you can rehearse your business pitch and ask for feedback from friends, but you have no direct control over whether potential investors emotionally connect with your vision)
- Make a mental note of the aspects that deserve more of your energy (e.g. practice pitching)
- Focus on the aspects that worry you, but are out of your control (e.g. the audience's personal history and their motivation to connect with your vision)
- Close your eyes, find a gentle and regular breathing pattern for a few moments and concentrate on the feeling that is evoked by the aspects you cannot control
- Simply observe the feelings with an attitude of curiosity and don't try to judge them as good or bad or push them away
- Stay with them for a while and open your mind to the possibility that the future will also bring unforeseen positive chances
- With your next exhale, because you cannot change them no matter how hard you try, make a deliberate decision to let your worries go for a while. The future is not created tomorrow. The future is created now
- Now you are more centered in the present moment, sit with your eyes closed for a few more breaths and direct your awareness to how you feel now
- With this presence, you direct your intentions and energy to the things that you can actually change today

# THE ENTREPRENEURIAL JOURNEY

As promised, we will get a bit more "technical" in this part of the book. Entrepreneurship is an evolving research field and, as we can see in the definition given by Bo Carlsson and colleagues, it encompasses various interconnected aspects of bringing bold ideas into existence:

**"Entrepreneurship refers primarily to an economic function that is carried out by individuals, entrepreneurs, acting independently or within organizations, to perceive and create new opportunities and to introduce their ideas into the market, under uncertainty, by making decisions about location, product design, resource use, institutions, and reward systems. The entrepreneurial activity and the entrepreneurial ventures are influenced by the socioeconomic environment and result ultimately in economic growth and human welfare."[1]**

We already touched on facets like economic growth, human welfare and some of the more practical aspects, such as business model-related decisions and product success. However, we are not yet ready to add mindfulness to our equation. The next two chapters will shed light on what it means to act entrepreneurial, the role of opportunities and the entrepreneurial journey from an internal perspective. We will dig deeper into the cognitive perspective on entrepreneurship, and talk about mindsets, purpose and why you need to take your *whole* self on the entrepreneurial journey.

PART 02

"Whether you succeed
or not is irrelevant,
there is no such thing.
Making your unknown known
is the important thing."

GEORGIA O'KEEFFE

# 03 Why Take Yourself on the Entrepreneurial Journey?

So what does it mean to "become" an entrepreneur? Why does it resonate with some people and why do they decide to embark on such a wild journey? And when they do, does that mean they have to stop being "themselves"? Many people are intimidated by the ideal of charismatic silicon valley entrepreneurs pitching for million-dollar investments to create billion-dollar businesses. For a good reason... Why not stay authentic and take on challenges that resonate with you and your capacity for driving change? You met Roger in the last chapter, and he seems quite down-to-earth, doesn't he? Many entrepreneurs start off with no clue what they are doing and figure it out along the way. It is part of the entrepreneurial journey and it certainly takes some courage. In this chapter, we will take a cognitive perspective from which to understand the *entrepreneurial journey* or the *entrepreneurial process*, if you prefer a more academic term.[2] Two core concepts in that regard are the *entrepreneurial mindset* and *entrepreneurial intentions*. Luckily, I got to talk to another expert in the field and we will conclude this chapter with a Deep Dive with entrepreneurial mindset advocate Dagmar Ylva Hattenberg. Dagmar is an organizational psychologist who dedicated her PhD research to investigating the entrepreneurial mindset.[3] Also, Dagmar and I recently published a conference paper on the role of mindsets in entrepreneurship and innovation.[4] How cool is that? Let's dive right into it and set the stage for Dagmar.

## A Dynamic Perspective on Human Behavior

I'll do a little fast forward to the interview with Dagmar right here. Dagmar suggests that "who *is* an entrepreneur?" is actually the wrong question to ask. Instead, we should ask "who *acts* entrepreneurial?" to understand the underlying entrepreneurial journey. A particular focus then lies on human action or human behavior in a wider sense. On a certain level of abstraction, entrepreneurship can be thought of as a dynamic set of specific behaviors. For example, doing market research, managing resources or connecting people with certain skills in a team. Taking this perspective allows us to draw on concepts from cognitive psychology. German psychologist Peter Gollwitzer provides a suitable framework with his *mindset theory of action phases*.[5] Generally speaking, the mindset theory of action phases suggests that planned human behavior can be divided into phases of *deliberation* or choosing a behavioral goal, *planning* possible actions to get there, actually *acting* on the goals and finally *evaluating* the process as well as its outcomes. In our minds, these distinct activities prime and require certain cognitive processes, which scholars refer to as *mindsets*. For example, the *deliberative mindset* and the *implemental mindset*. We will have a closer look at these concepts in the next section.

Another interesting aspect of his theory is the importance of implementation intentions. In subsequent empirical research, Peter Gollwitzer and other researchers found that clearly defining *when*, *where* and *how* to act on a chosen goal has positive effects on actually achieving the respective goal.[6] So, this is a simple, yet powerful tool for becoming more consistent in achieving goals. Several mechanisms contribute to the effectiveness of implementation intentions. For example, they can increase the chance of actual initiation of striving for a goal; and they can shield continuous goal pursuit from unexpected influences, preventing behavioral disengagement caused by unexpected setbacks. What does that mean for us? If you are serious about something that you made a decision on, do not only decide *what* to do. For instance, if you genuinely want to start a business, you should sit down and map out a plan about *when, where* and *how* you want to perform certain activities. Reality will still get you and you will have to adapt, but cognitively it can make a crucial difference. By the way, if you are familiar with the book *Atomic Habits* by James Clear, this is one of the theories behind it![7] It also worked quite well for me. In 2020 I mapped out ten blog posts, which provided the initial storyline for this book including publishing dates, topics and potential interview partners on a train ride. And here we are! It is something that I mentally turned back to and that got me through moments in which I lost motivation. I wanted to get out and do handstands with my friends instead! However, it helped me to maintain the volition to do what I needed to do.

You will read more about my struggles in Chapter 6. Did I always stick to it? Of course not! For example, I had to wait to get interview appointments and then to get feedback on the transcripts. However, these are often the things out of our control (remember the exercise from last chapter?). Obviously, there will always be what scholars call the *intention-behavior gap* and there are various internal, as well as external reasons for this gap. Anyway, for me it worked pretty well as an internal game

plan. Then, what about that mindset thingy? Making decisions, planning their implementation and acting on them are cognitively distinct tasks, which require our minds to be in different states. Let's have a closer look at those mindset concepts.

## The Deliberative and Implemental Mindset

In simple terms, deliberating whether or not a goal is worth pursuing involves the assessment of its *desirability* and *feasibility*. What's in it for me? Will I enjoy working towards my new goal? Do I actually believe in my abilities to turn it into reality? We will discuss *desirability* as well as *feasibility* considerations and deliberating intentions in more detail in the next chapter. Here is a general overview of Peter Gollwitzer's mindset theory of action phases.[8]

Peter Gollwitzer suggests that the deliberative mindset, which is primed by choosing between possible paths of action, is characterized by four specific aspects. First, the deliberative mindset is deployed whenever you become intensely involved with evaluating your desires. In order to promote this task, a cognitive tuning toward information relevant to the issues of feasibility and desirability gets activated. Additionally, the deliberative mindset entails an orientation towards precise and unbiased processing of information. Lastly, it implies an open-mindedness or increased receptivity to information in general. By contrast, an Implemental Mindset is activated by a readily made decision or goal implementation. It plays a major role in facilitating goal achievement. Hence, the theory suggests that it is characterized by a cognitive turning towards internal and external cues that guide your course of action towards goal attainment. Because it should originate whenever you move effectively towards goal attainment, it is somewhat supported by closed-mindedness to information that could trigger a re-evaluation of the goal that is being pursued, a re-evaluation of the planned route towards goal attainment, or any self-evaluation in a wider sense. Peter Gollwitzer's theory is quite generally applicable and does not specifically address entrepreneurial issues. Luckily, other scholars have already done this job for us. Let's have a look at how these ideas translate into the world of entrepreneurs and hence, the entrepreneurial journey.

## The Entrepreneurial Journey

As we saw in the initial definition of entrepreneurship, opportunities are at the core of entrepreneurial activity. In order to act on a perceived opportunity, aspiring entrepreneurs need to be convinced of the positive outcome of doing so and their personal ability to successfully act on it. In entrepreneurship research, many studies confirmed this idea. Most notably, a recent study by Servane Delanoë-Gueguen and Alain Fayolle specifically used Peter Gollwitzer's mindset theory of action phases to get a clearer picture of the entrepreneurial journey.[9] On the next page, Figure 4 visualizes how the processes discussed in the last section translate into entrepreneurial behavior.

Are you getting clearer about the things that drive you? Is a value hypothesis taking shape? Did you start researching potential customer segments or scribble a logo? Congratulations, once your actions shift from pure gathering of information to more concrete tasks, you cross what Servane Delanoë-Gueguen and Alain Fayolle call the *entrepreneurial Rubicon* and stop being a *nascent entrepreneur*. Basically, deep down you started your entrepreneurial journey and became an aspiring entrepreneur. Yet, when we talk about the importance of entrepreneurship for society, we obviously talk about thriving and growing ventures that create employment and solutions to pressing issues. Here, it gets more complicated. Delanoë-Gueguen and Fayolle showed that the motivational aspects are important in the stage before aspiring entrepreneurs start to act on their entrepreneurial goals. This involves the deliberative mindset, as discussed in the last section. Once aspiring entrepreneurs cross the entrepreneurial Rubicon, implemental aspects get more significant. Here, it is about volition and being able to implement one's intentions. This is why implementation intentions are important. Entering the startup-phase, scholars assume that entrepreneurs re-enter a deliberative mindset and evaluate future growth plans.

To sum this up... We know that entrepreneurship can be thought of as a dynamic set of behaviors and that these behaviors can be differentiated into deliberation, planning, acting and evaluating. Furthermore, these behaviors prime and require deliberative or implemental mindsets. In the context of entrepreneurship, we know that motivation plays a more important role in the preactional phase, while volition gets more crucial later on. Remember that entrepreneurship is a marathon, after all! Lastly, we learned that clear implementation intentions can help the entrepreneur maintain volition. So much for the theory... And what about the entrepreneurial mindset, which has even been termed "the essence of being entrepreneurial"?[10] We talked about the role of mindsets in the entrepreneurial journey, but is it the same thing? Let's dig deeper on that issue with Dagmar!

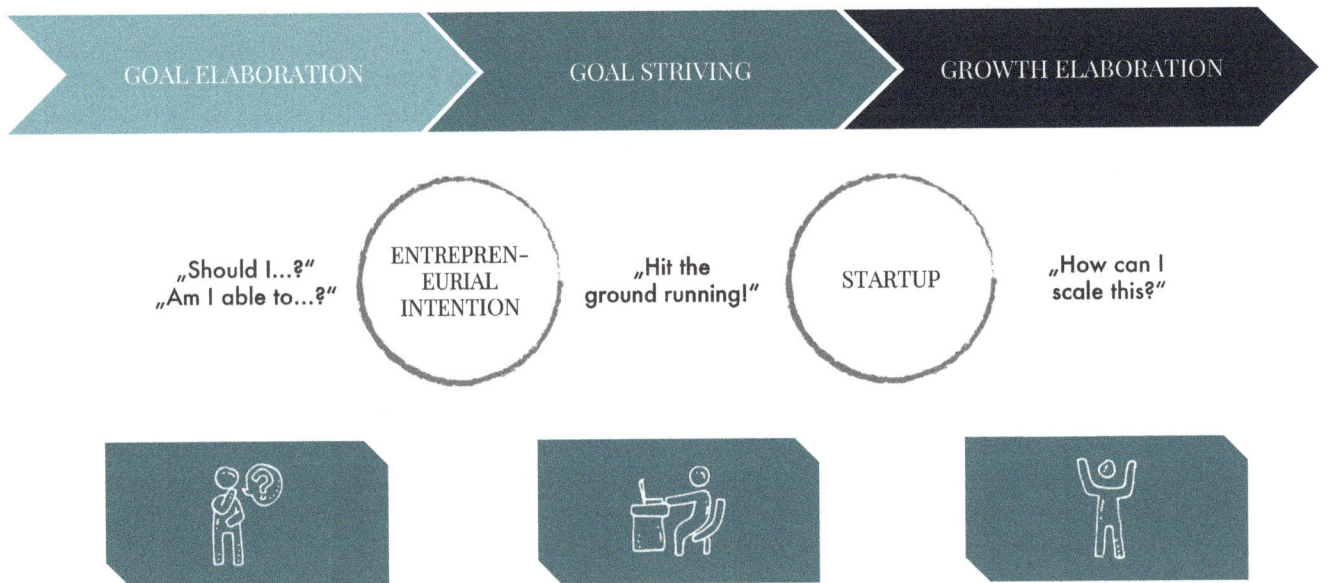

GOAL ELABORATION | GOAL STRIVING | GROWTH ELABORATION

„Should I...?"
„Am I able to...?"

ENTREPREN-
EURIAL
INTENTION

„Hit the
ground running!"

STARTUP

„How can I
scale this?"

*Figure 4: The simplified entrepreneurial journey. Based on Delanoë-Gueguen and Fayolle (2019).*

48

# Deep Dive

A Conversation with Dagmar Ylva Hattenberg,
the Curious Entrepreneurial Mindset Advocate

Malte: Hey Dagmar! I am so happy that you are going to share your insights with me. I am excited to hear your perspective and where you stand with your research. Let's get right into it and start with yourself. What was your motivation for investigating and advocating the entrepreneurial mindset during your PhD?

Dagmar: So, before I started the PhD I was already starting to figure out what I wanted in terms of my research topic. I knew I wanted to pursue a PhD, but I was not sure yet about what kind of topic. I have a background in organizational psychology and I was always interested in the individual. Why are individuals so passionate about the things they are doing? What creates such passion? Those kinds of questions. And, after applying for a PhD in organizational entrepreneurship, I had to find a way to combine that. I was digging deeper into the existing knowledge and figured out that I was really interested in what is going on in people's minds. At that point, I did not really have a definition of what the mind is or what a person feels or thinks, but I realized that this was what mostly interested me. Because that is what drives a person to act, right? I was working in a company at that time and I realized there were people who would take entrepreneurial initiatives and people who would not. And I was wondering why. Then I came across work on the entrepreneurial mindset and intentions. This led me to dig deeper on the whole issue.

Malte: Well, that sounds like a good reason to get curious! And did the concept of mindsets help you in understanding why certain individuals take entrepreneurial action and others do not?

Dagmar: Well, yes and no. It's funny, because I mostly start my papers with this quote: "'It's wrong to look on who is the entrepreneur. It's actually the wrong question to ask. The right question is — Who acts entrepreneurial?" That put things in perspective for me. I think everybody has an entrepreneurial mindset! It's really the will to use it that differentiates us. I like this quote, because it does not suggest that one person is entrepreneurial and the other one is not. It is really the choice to act on an entrepreneurial issue that matters. And that gave me more insights into the passions and motivations of people. Because it shows that some people are willing and able to act entrepreneurial. Some are willing but not able. Whereas other people are able, but not willing, and people can develop pieces of that.

Malte: I like that! You are in the process of publishing a paper, which examines definitions of the entrepreneurial mindset and how it is distinct from other cognitive phenomena in entrepreneurship research. So, what is your definition?

Dagmar: Yes, so for academic purposes I am using the definition from Shepherd and colleagues.[11] In summary, it is the willingness and ability of individuals to sense, seize and act on an opportunity. So to see that there is something going on that could be an opportunity and also really the activity of acknowledging the opportunity, grabbing it with both hands and taking action. What do I need to realize this opportunity? Do I need help? Do I need resources? And always with the focus of gaining something out of this. So not just driving yourself wildly into something. Really with a focus on personal development, financial or any sort of gain.

Malte: Then, how can you influence that mindset? How do you get individuals to sense opportunities and act on them?

Dagmar: That is a really good question and I have a paper coming out on this as well. Based on my experience from the corporate context, I think that it is actually pretty easy to stimulate people to act entrepreneurial. Because what most people need in my opinion is simply the support to do so! So when people are already willing, what they need is to be enabled to do so. That could be in terms of resources, that could be in terms of a sparring partner or that could be in terms of time to perform the activity. It is a little bit harder if people are not that willing. But you can still stimulate them to be entrepreneurial. People always think that entrepreneurship is about these gigantic big initiatives. It has to be that million dollar success, but it doesn't have to be. Sometimes change is not that big and can have a huge impact on the environment. I think the same applies to students and people in general. I think it is fairly easy to stimulate people in their ability but also their willingness to be entrepreneurial.

Malte: That sounds very promising. David, one of my master's thesis students, already reached out to you on that matter, as far as I know. He wants to conceptualize a framework for how universities can stimulate the entrepreneurial mindset more systematically. But there might be a downside of that. Recently, I talked to my friend Rogelio, who is an entrepreneur himself. We talked a lot about entrepreneurial well-being and getting through the hard times of being an entrepreneur. On the one hand, we want to stimulate the entrepreneurial mindset, but on the other hand, we do not want people to be too engaged. I am really thinking about burnout, depression and these kinds of issues. We want to ignite them and not set them on fire, right? What is your take on that?

Dagmar: Well, I think this is quite interesting. I have done this ethnographic study, where I followed people for almost one year in a company to see how they act when they come across certain initiatives. It is a highly stimulated entrepreneurial context. People get really pushed to become entrepreneurial. I came up with four archetypes of entrepreneurs in a company. I noticed that those who were too engaged really tried to be aware of every project going on — almost running around like headless chickens. They almost had a fear of missing out and basically forgot that they are also a person outside of this entrepreneurial act. It is something that might result in burnout or them being super stressed out and it often gives them more worries rather than doing them any good. I think that they sensed an opportunity, they seized it and they are acting on it, but they kind of forgot about the gain part! I think there should always be something to gain for themselves. Because that gives some kind of balance! You also focus on what you can get out of it. You need to find that balance between you and the entrepreneur. This is an idea and I don't know if it is true, but it is something that I will look into.

Malte: That is so curious. It reminds me of the aspects I talked about with Rogelio. He said that he always gave his 100% for the company at the beginning and basically forgot about himself. He did not maintain this balance of his needs as a person and him as an entrepreneur as a result. He suggested that entrepreneurship is a marathon and not a sprint, and that entrepreneurs should rather get ready for a long and slow ride. That requires maintaining a balance right from the beginning. We did not discuss this distinction between outcome and process, but I think it is a really interesting perspective. The outcomes of your venture should fulfill you!

Dagmar: Exactly, the point that you raise about your own needs is something that we tend not to focus on in Western countries. Instead, we focus on the *flow* of doing things. So when you are for instance setting up something entrepreneurial, we praise those people. It is very good to be in a flow and we praise those people who give 120% rather than 100%. But that actually comes at quite a high cost. You are losing a bit of yourself, which could result in depression, burnout or stress. And it is indeed because we put too much focus on this flow and on hard work and dedication.

Malte: True! I am still exploring this interplay of entrepreneurship and mindfulness. At some level, they seem to contradict each other, but then I think there is a lot of potential. Of course, you have to work hard and give your 100%. If you don't take things forward, nobody will. Yet, at the same time, you should not forget about yourself. At the end of a day, it comes down to running your venture in a more sustainable way.

Dagmar: Actually, I would never say that mindfulness and entrepreneurship are contradictory. Mindfulness is more like a great resource to become a stronger entrepreneur. It helps you to focus, to become more effective and more efficient. Rather than being all over the place, which is often a problem, in my opinion. That results in stress. Whereas mindfulness reduces stress because it helps you to center on your own self and realize the gains that you are aiming for. So, it totally makes sense to look into entrepreneurship and mindfulness together. It is very logical. I never thought about it before, but it makes a lot of sense.

Malte: Well, thank you for encouraging my endeavor! It seems like we are both on a mission to advocate similar ideas. Regarding the entrepreneurial mindset, I admire what you are doing. I think it is so important to ignite people's minds, especially young ones, with role models, ideas and the right environment in which it is OK to try things and fail. But we need to take it from there and support them in taking themselves on the journey. Your insights definitely got us a little bit closer to do that!

## In a Nutshell...

In this chapter, we got to understand the entrepreneurial journey in more detail and explored how it relates to important aspects of it like our mindsets and intentions. According to Dean Shepherd and his colleagues, the entrepreneurial mindset reflects an individual's willingness and ability to recognize and realize opportunities of creating entrepreneurial ventures.[12] Hence, it arguably covers aspects of deliberative and implemental mindsets. It is a holistic view of entrepreneurs' cognitive, emotional and behavioral processes in response to these opportunities. I feel that Dagmar explained nicely why we all have the potential to become entrepreneurs and why entrepreneurs should not forget about the personal gain part. Because another crucial point to keep in mind is that the entrepreneurial journey is inherently *goal-directed*. As we just heard, it might be tempting to get lost in striving for these goals. In combination with the insights from the last chapter and the Deep Dive with Rogelio, I hope it is becoming clearer why you should really take your *whole* self on the entrepreneurial journey. Why are you personally starting this? What is in it for you? Don't get too consumed in your cause. Self-responsibility begins with appreciating that you have needs, such as financial security, periods of rest and recovery or personal development. Own them and celebrate your successes!

However, there is still the marathon part of things, which is really about walking the fine line between grit and self-abandonment. You will definitely need volition to get you through the hard times and a clear implementation intention might be a valuable tool for that.

So, are you feeling brave today? Really, how serious are you about starting a venture or continuing your journey? In the first chapter, I introduced an exercise about getting closer to the things that move you and some personal boundaries that might determine how you will act on them. Let's get a little bit more serious here. What about coming up with an actual implementation intention? If you are already running a business or mentoring entrepreneurs, feel free to adapt it to another aspect of your life! What about a dedicated mindfulness training program for your protégés or team, for example? Anyway, be aware that the next exercise might have a serious impact on your life...

# I Dare You:

## Manifest Your Wholehearted Journey!

- Take some time, your genuine attention and a blank sheet of paper
- Draw a horizontal line about a third of the way up
- Draw an orthogonal vertical line at the left side of the first line (you should have a simple graph now)
- Imagine the horizontal line to be the timeline of your life in the next two to three years
- Imagine the vertical line as your achievements in that time (there is only a way up, you see!)
- Get wild! What are the things you will achieve and how do they build upon one another? Map them out as events over the next two to three years
- How, where and when will you act to get there? What are the actions and milestones that will help you to convert your vision into action?
- What will be the big impact that you are trying to make at the end?
- Don't forget to take yourself on the journey! What keeps you motivated and in balance?
- Be creative... Illustrate and connect everything to come up with a wild and engaging journey
- Cultivate a bias towards action and take the next implementable step!

„He who has a why
to live can bear
almost any
how.”

FRIEDRICH NIETZSCHE

# 04 On Intentions, Purpose and Ikigai

In the last chapter, we talked about the entrepreneurial journey, the role of mindsets and intentions. However, we did not get into much detail about the cognitive processes behind the formation of intentions. How do people make a judgement about the desirability and feasibility of potential courses of action? In this chapter, we will dig deeper into the hearts and minds of entrepreneurs. Making our way from intentions to goals, we will talk about purpose in life and how Eastern philosophy, including the Japanese concept of Ikigai, might help you to enjoy your entrepreneurial journey. Friedrich Nietzsche probably has a point with the quote, which opened this chapter. We will see! Lastly, we will slowly venture into the world of meditation on our expedition towards Entrepreneurial Mindfulness.

## The Startup Starts Within You

We learned that sensing, seizing and acting on entrepreneurial opportunities is an essential part of acting entrepreneurial. But how do human beings decide if a certain situation is an opportunity worth pursuing rather than a threat? Let's face it... Few people are entirely comfortable with constant change, ambiguity and the turbulent mess of our dynamic global environment. Nevertheless, social startup success stories like TOMS Shoes, a company that started donating a pair of shoes for every pair you buy and today donates $1 for every $3 they make[13] or Too Good To Go, a movement that set out to reduce food waste[14] show that there are huge opportunities for positive impact through purpose-driven entrepreneurship.

With the right vision in mind, humans can truly move mountains! But why do some people decide to act on such a vision to become entrepreneurs while others don't? Looking back at the theories form last chapter, we learned that this decision mainly depends on two elements — *desirability* as well as *feasibility* considerations. If I think that there is something in it for me, I might enjoy it and I am capable of acting on the potential goal effectively, I might thus form an *entrepreneurial intention*. A true turning point in understanding the decision to start new ventures was Norris Krueger's finding that opportunity recognition is an intentional process and the *theory of planned behavior* might be a suitable tool for empirically investigating that suggestion.[15] Norris was also a co-author with Dagmar and me on mindsets in entrepreneurship and innovation, and he is highly dedicated to supporting entrepreneurial ecosystems all over the globe. Definitely check out one of his many talks on the topic.

Anyway, let's take a look at the very accessible, straightforward theory of planned behavior from Professor Icek Ajzen. To give you an idea how widely applicable it is, the last time I checked, he was being cited twice as often as 2017 Economics Nobel Prize laureate Richard Thaler (the nudging guy).[16] Alright, now let's have a look at the theory and how it might help us to understand the inner world of *nascent entrepreneurs*.

## The Hearts and Minds of Entrepreneurs

Professor Ajzen suggests that the closest cognitive

antecedent to actually observable behavior is an intention.[17] So far, this is no big news, since we already talked about it in the last chapter. However, his theory allows us to dig a little bit deeper into the hearts and minds entrepreneurs, because it provides more detailed insights on the formation of intentions. So, what's going on before intentions are set? Or in Norris Krueger's words, what influences entrepreneurial *desirability* and *feasibility* considerations? According to the theory of planned behavior, this can be summarized in three elements. First of all, the *attitude* towards behavior plays an important role. This can be value expectancy measures, as in the question "what's in it for me?" But there are also also experiential considerations: "will I enjoy the ride?" Nevertheless, that alone is not enough to explain the deliberation process of setting a behavioral intention. Human beings rarely act in social isolation. Our social environment influences all of us. More precisely, the perception of our social environment and what people might expect of us. This is a matter of *perceived social norms*. What do your friends think about you pursuing this idea on your mind and quitting a well-paid job? Or your parents or partner? The first two aspects can be thought of as *desirability* considerations. Lastly, *feasibility* considerations give us the entire picture. *Perceived behavioral control* is the third variable in the equation. Do I think that I can really pull this thing off? Do I believe in my own abilities? Another academic term to describe this is *self-efficacy*. By the way, a study from 2020 showed that entrepreneurial self-efficacy can be enhanced by growth mindset interventions, which we discussed in the first part of the book.[18]

The theory of planned behavior has provided a solid theoretical framework for many studies that investigate entrepreneurial intentions. For example, in 2013 Teemu Kautonen and his colleagues published a study in which they took two waves of survey data from the working-age population of Finland.[19] By taking two consecutive surveys separated by several years with the same group of people, they were able to show that enough of the entrepreneurial intentions had been transformed into entrepreneurial behavior to show a statistically significant correlation. In simple terms, in many cases those people who planned to become entrepreneurs consequently did so. Hence, they were able to predict entrepreneurial behavior before it was actually observable. Let's take these insights and go back to the Entrepreneurial Mindfulness Diagram. Is it more than just a fancy picture? I certainly think so! When we keep *attitudes* towards entrepreneurial behavior, *social norms* and *perceived behavioral control* in mind, how does that relate to the diagram?

You are smart, so I guess you might have figured it out already... But we will still have a look at the four elements that are at the core of the diagram. Let's start with love! At the end of the day, this is nothing else than an experiential attitude. Do you expect to enjoy the activities that will get you to where you want to go? Of course, you will not enjoy all of it... We all have to do our taxes and you might not be a born public speaker. However, there should be a considerable proportion of the activities that somehow get you into a state of *flow*, as positive psychologist Mihaly Csikszentmihalyi would call it.[20] Sometimes, I would prefer to go out and practice Yoga in the park nearby, but overall I enjoy writing and letting my ideas flow to create this book. Therefore, it is not the worst trade-off for me.

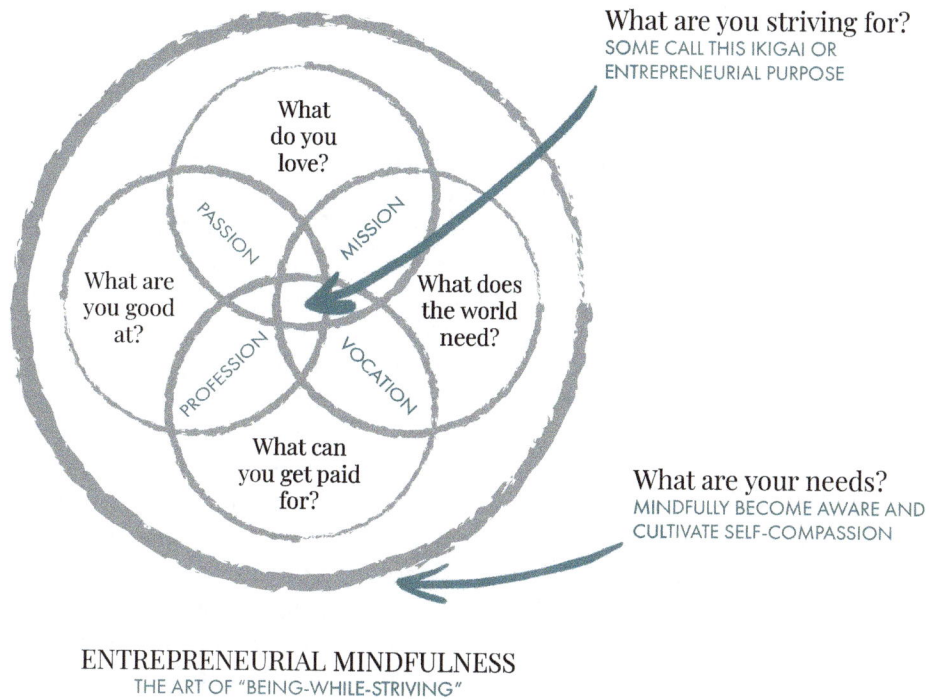

What are you striving for?
SOME CALL THIS IKIGAI OR
ENTREPRENEURIAL PURPOSE

What do you love?

PASSION

MISSION

What are you good at?

PROFESSION

VOCATION

What does the world need?

What can you get paid for?

What are your needs?
MINDFULLY BECOME AWARE AND
CULTIVATE SELF-COMPASSION

ENTREPRENEURIAL MINDFULNESS
THE ART OF "BEING-WHILE-STRIVING"

*Figure 5: Entrepreneurial Mindfulness Diagram. Based on García and Miralles (2017).*

That leaves us with three other elements in the diagram. Let's continue with "What can you get paid for?" Here, we are talking about a value-expectancy consideration. At the end of the day, we all have to pay our rent, whether we are a founder, employee or student. So, it is only reasonable to ask this question. While the intention of such an infographic is to simplify a more complex idea, I'm quite confident that this one is compatible with actual science. This suggestion is reinforced by looking at the question "What are you good at?" With regard to the theory of planned behavior, this is a matter of *perceived behavioral control*. Do my personal skills and qualities allow me to confidently start the venture under consideration? Looking back at the interview on the entrepreneurial mindset with Dagmar, this is really about the perceived ability to act on opportunities. It gets a little bit more complicated when it comes to the question "What does the world need?" While this is connected to the *social norms* construct, it is taking a rather wider perspective. Typically, studies about entrepreneurial intentions examine the immediate social environment, such as family, friends or colleagues. Therefore, here we might deviate slightly from previous research. However, I want to bear in mind that we are talking about Entrepreneurial Mindfulness; I believe that the idea of an *entrepreneurial purpose* should not be underestimated. Let me build on Rogelio and Dagmar's insights and explain why.

## Purpose in Life Is a Choice – Make It!

If you ask 10 people what they think the purpose of life is, you might get 10 different answers... And all these answers might be true for that specific person in their specific context. So, let's begin with something more agreeable. According to Patrick McKnight and Todd Kashdan from George Mason University, purpose in life is best understood as a *cognitive process*.[21] The two authors suggest that while most people *can* have a purpose (given their general cognitive capability), not all human beings *do* have one. Basically, it is a narrative about yourself that you have to find and define yourself. In that sense, I believe that finding purpose is an intentional process in its own right. If you succeed, the benefits might be manifold. In their study, McKnight and Kashdan suggest that purpose positively affects longevity, general health, and physical and mental well-being. They suggest that people who found a purpose in life likely live healthier and happier lives. Not too irrelevant to the things Rogelio shared in the Deep Dive about entrepreneurial well-being, right? In that sense, purpose is suggested to be a vital, self-organizing life aim, which organizes and stimulates goals. Therefore, it also manages behaviors and provides a source of meaning. It directs the goals you set in life and consequently affects daily decisions. Living in harmony with that purpose provides an ongoing source of meaning through pursuing goals and realizing them. And here the circle closes... Goals are central to and produced by purpose. Purpose in turn is tightly knit to a person's identity, which depends on the experiences drawn from pursuing, achieving and failing to accomplish goals. What are the lessons that you learn out of your failures and successes? Don't live to fulfill your goals. Let your goals be a source of fulfillment! I believe that it comes down to the recurring role of self-awareness. McKnight and Kashdan also discuss awareness as a central theme in their conceptual framework. In this context, awareness reflects the extent to which an individual is aware and can express her or his purpose.

Furthermore, they indicate that awareness might reinforce the bond between purpose and positive life outcomes such as health and well-being. They refer to a study that builds on... right, *mindfulness!*[22] The study suggests that mindfulness concerns a clear awareness of one's inner and outer worlds, such as thoughts, emotions, sensations, actions, or surroundings. More about that in the next chapter.

At this point, we can assume that having a purpose and acting in harmony with it is good for you. Does your purpose have to affect the entire world? Of course not... However, I believe that it is a good place to start the search! Why not turn this into an exercise of creative confidence? You can still get active in your local community. However, do not zoom in too much. Someone with a purpose should not be confused with someone living a hedonistic way of life. Purpose is explicitly defined as a *higher order* cognitive process.[23] A hedonistic person lives with a goal-directed motivation, but the fact that the motivation stems from a drive of satisfying personal desires stands in contrast with the notion of a higher order cognitive process. Consequently, purpose in life should have certain components *outside* of your own life. Whether you want to change the world or your neighborhood is up to you!

So, what about *purpose-driven entrepreneurship*? According to Kai Hockerts from Copenhagen Business School, the main purpose of existence for *social purpose business ventures* is to create external social benefits.[24] Again, I don't mind which term you end up using. From my point of view, they seem quite compatible and depend on the perspective you take. For the purpose of this book, I choose the term purpose-driven entrepreneurship and I am implying a social cause. Most importantly, I suggest

you don't miss out on staying connected to your purpose when you set out for the entrepreneurial marathon! It might well be the thing that gets you through challenging times and answers a crucial question, "*Why* am I doing this?"

## Some Call This Ikigai?

The curious reader might have spotted another word in the diagram. Yes, some people equate life purpose with the Japanese concept of *Ikigai*. If you have read the book Ikigai by Héctor Garcias and Francesc Miralles, you might have seen a Venn diagram that is pretty similar to the one in this book.[25] However, if you are like me, you might have noted the absence of hands-on guidance on how to define that very purpose. After reading and writing a lot about these topics, I came to the conclusion that it is not something that a book can teach you in any case. It comes through intention, awareness, experience, self-inquiry, contemplation, meditation and time, time, time... Nevertheless, according to Japanologist Nicholas Kemp, the Ikigai Venn Diagram was actually developed in the context of purpose-driven entrepreneurship in the West.[26] Nicholas Kemp suggests that the original Japanese concept of Ikigai is instead something that has to be experienced in things like building harmonious relationships, finding flow in hobbies, or by expressing your creativity, gratitude and helping others in your life roles or by cultivating presence in daily rituals and celebrating small joys of life (mindfulness anyone?). From my point of view, these activities and attitudes are necessary to get yourself through the tides of life, entrepreneur or not. They are crucial to our well-being, and they definitely enrich our human experience. Essentially, it is about *how* you take the ride. So, let's talk about mindfulness!

## In a Nutshell...

Changemakers who are empowered by a strong sense of purpose and who have a vision of how to turn it into reality can truly move mountains. Purpose in life determines the goals we set and how we act on them. So, it's strongly related to our intentions, which we also got to understand better in this chapter. You will know what to do when your Yoga teacher asks you to set an intention for the practice next time. Furthermore, purpose seems to be an important contributor to a happy and fulfilled (entrepreneurial) life. Most importantly, it is a choice! Are you aware of your strengths, passions and experiences? Do you contemplate the narrative of your life? I believe that it comes down to cultivating self-awareness and turning this into purposeful action. Whether you call it purpose or Ikigai, make sure to spend time contemplating on the path you are taking. Make it a deliberate, conscious and wholehearted choice. You only have this one life.

Do you need some guidance on the contemplation part? The exercise at the end of this chapter might help you to strengthen this important aspect of your entrepreneurial journey. In the last chapter, I provided an exercise in which I asked you to reflect on the things that drive you and how this could manifest itself in an entrepreneurial journey. This exercise goes in a similar direction, but it takes an entirely different approach. Instead of looking for answers in active reflection, we are dwelling on the question "what is my path?" Rather than solving this riddle with active thinking, we try not to think and cultivate an attitude of curiosity. We take the observer's seat for the answers our subconscious mind might bring to us. It is about cultivating curiosity and presence! I suggest that you revisit this question on a regular basis to constantly check if you are still on a path that feels right for you. It is essentially about stopping the autopilot for a while. Also, you might be totally unclear about your path, or it might change over time. That's fine! We have new experiences, our attitudes change, and so might our purpose. In his book *Wherever You Go, There You Are*, Jon Kabat-Zinn writes that our personal vision has to be renewed every day and it has to be right in front of us because mindfulness also requires this level of awareness and clear intention.[27] Less talk, more action (or rather *non-action*)! If you are new to meditation, this is a nice, soft entry. There's no implicit expectation of immediate inner silence or anything like that. You still have your question to cling to.

# I Dare You:

## Contemplate Your Purpose!

- Let's (re)connect with our direction and practice to enjoy the ride
- Make a deliberate decision to create some space for non-doing
- Find a comfortable sitting or lying position
- Spend one minute in silence and mentally arrive wherever you are
- Simply follow the sensation of your breath for 10 deep, nourishing inhales and exhales
- Maintain a steady, calm breath and set your mind on a question that resonates with you for 5, 10 or 15 minutes
- Begin contemplating where you are and where you truly want to be
- Questions you can dwell on:
    - What is my purpose in life?
    - What is my vision for the future?
    - Where am I going?
    - What do I truly want?
    - What do I want my legacy to be?
- Just stay with the question using your curiosity and do not try to look for answers with your thinking mind
- After you finish the formal meditation part, you may want to reflect on it with your thinking mind and take a critical look at where things are going with your life
- Again, there is no right or wrong, and not having a decisive answer is totally fine
- The moment you take the time to dwell on the question is already a part of the journey

# INFUSING MINDFULNESS

Time for a brief recap. In the first part of the book, we discussed three challenges that entrepreneurs are facing. They are challenged to create a positive impact, need to get a viable business running and should stay sane and healthy during their entrepreneurial marathon. In Part Two of the book, we got to understand the entrepreneurial journey, intentions and mindsets in more detail. Furthermore, we discussed why it might be a good idea to maintain a strong sense of purpose and contribute to "something bigger" than oneself. Now, I would like to add the concept of mindfulness to the equation.

As entrepreneurs, we engage in goal-directed behavior to create our vision of the future, which is our common denominator. We dwell on things that do not exist yet because we are convinced that they should come into existence. Mindfulness, however, is essentially about staying aware of the present moment. Let's explore this apparent paradox and the potential of resolving it by cultivating a mode of *Being-while-Striving*. In the next two chapters, you will be introduced to mindfulness, how it relates to meditation, exciting scientific findings about its effects and an eight-week Entrepreneurial Mindfulness self-experiment. I believe that the future can be created from the present moment and that we can cultivate this mode of *Being-while-Striving*. Moreover, I believe that this mode comes with many positive effects for entrepreneurs and society, which strongly benefits from their actions.

## PART 03

"Half an hour's meditation each day is essential, except when you are busy. Then a full hour is needed."

SAINT FRANCIS DE SALES

# 05 Mindfulness and Its Potential for Entrepreneurship

When they are handling the external challenge of starting a new venture, entrepreneurs must handle the internal challenges of coping with ambiguity, stress and decision making under extreme uncertainty. Additionally, society faces a multitude of challenges and relies on innovative entrepreneurs to deal with them. Racial inequality, global pandemics, climate change, plastic waste... you name it. What if something could support entrepreneurs to be more successful in dealing with all these challenges? I believe that systematically integrating the cultivation of mindfulness and compassion through meditation practices into the domain of entrepreneurship might be that very thing.

SOCIETY INVESTS
EDUCATION, TRAINING, ETC...

ENTREPRENEUR RETURNS
EMPLOYMENT, SOLUTIONS, ETC...

*Figure 6: A symbiosis of society and entrepreneurs.*

## Four Propositions on a Symbiotic Relationship

In the process of reading, writing and having conversations about entrepreneurship and mindfulness, I came to realize with more clarity that entrepreneurs and society actually form a symbiotic relationship. On the one hand, society relies on innovative solutions from entrepreneurs, as discussed in Part One. On the other hand, the entrepreneurial journey is challenging, and future entrepreneurs benefit from education, training, investments and networks. Dagmar already shared some insights about honing the entrepreneurial mindset and we will go into more detail about entrepreneurial education and training in Part Four. At this stage, I will add the concept of mindfulness to the equation and propose four ways in which I believe it positively influences the symbiosis I just described. The following four propositions are partly inspired by academic research, partly based on the Deep Dives from this book and spiced up with my own thoughts:[1]

- **Proposition 1** — integrating meditation and mindfulness practice into entrepreneurial training and education will have a positive effect on entrepreneurs' pursuit of a socially- or sustainability-driven purpose
- **Proposition 2** — integrating meditation and mindfulness practice into entrepreneurial training and education will help entrepreneurs to effectively turn their purpose into goals and actions
- **Proposition 3** — integrating meditation and mindfulness practice into entrepreneurial training and education will have a

positive effect on entrepreneurs' decision making skills

- **Proposition 4** — integrating meditation and mindfulness practice into entrepreneurial training and education will support entrepreneurs in taking care of their well-being and mental health

In combination, I believe that integrating mindfulness into entrepreneurship education and training has amazing potential to create and sustain impactful change for all of us. It will create entrepreneurs who care about the challenges our society has, who are ready to act on them, who make better decisions and who feel well while bringing about sustainable change. That doesn't sound too bad to me!

## Meditation and Mindfulness

Some people say that meditation is amongst the oldest human activities (or rather non-activities) that go beyond securing our survival, like hunting, maintaining social ties or taking care of a shelter. We will have a look at some more formal practices at the end of this chapter. Yet, it might have started in a much simpler way. Sitting by the fire, looking into the flames and gently drifting into a state of *being* might be one of the oldest forms of meditation. Fun fact: author Yuval Noah Harari, who knows quite a lot about human history, once did a *Vipassana* or silence meditation retreat for 60 consecutive days.[2] Maybe there is something about the human experience and meditation.

However, it seems to me like Western society has lost the appreciation of simply *being* and experiencing with gratitude the things that unfold within and around us. Sure, social media and increasing screen times are the easy culprits to blame. However, to me the issue seems to go much deeper. I feel that we fundamentally shifted our focus and aspirations away from the things that truly matter, such as finding meaningful connections with the people who are dear to us or savoring the little moments that make us smile. However, slowly, people in the West are rediscovering the Eastern ways of life, such as Buddhism and Hinduism, in which the traditions of meditation and mindfulness remained much more common. Yoga studios are popping up around the world in which people begin to reconnect with their inner world, and Yoga teacher training are increasingly common among Western students.

Furthermore, from a scientific perspective, the relevance of meditation and mindfulness in Western culture experienced an important shift in the 1970s. That was when passionate scholar of Eastern traditions Jon Kabat-Zinn developed a more standardized mindfulness and meditation approach in the form of an eight-week training.[3] The Mindfulness Based Stress Reduction (MBSR) program gave science something more testable and resulted in a rich stream of supporting research. According to a review of mindfulness studies by Jenny Gu and colleagues, mindfulness-based interventions can have a positive effect on many important issues such as anxiety, depression, stress, chronic pain and even overall quality of life.[4] Some studies also report positive effects on social well-being. In summary, it covers the entire spectrum of challenges discussed in Chapter 2.

We will have a closer look at entrepreneurship-specific well-being mechanisms later. For now, we can assume that cultivating mindfulness through meditation is good for you! The MBSR program takes participants through various forms of formal meditation techniques, involving a commitment to daily individual meditation practice and including informal practice, such as mindful eating. MBSR involves meditation techniques like body scan, seated meditation and meditation experienced through gentle movements. The program aims at helping you to navigate the challenges of daily life more mindfully and remain calm even in stressful situations. I will introduce the program in more depth in the next chapter. This systematic approach to mindfulness and meditation practices also allowed scholars to derive more concise definitions.

A widely applied mindfulness conceptualization in the Western scientific context was developed by Kirk Brown and Richard Ryan.[5] In their view, mindfulness is a unique combination of three facets. One of these facets is a certain *awareness* of the present moment and what is happing within ourselves and the world around us. For example, we could be experiencing emotions, thoughts, body sensations or social interactions. Furthermore, mindfulness is characterized by intentionally paying *attention* to these events and experiences. Ideally, for a sustained period of time. Hence, it is a particular combination of being aware of and paying attention to the present moment. Lastly, mindfulness implies an attitude of *curiosity* and *openness*. We don't try to push away difficult emotions or we don't run away from difficult conversations. It's quite the opposite of "good vibes only". We rather develop an ability to witness these experiences as a calm observer. We become adventurous explorers of our internal world. Do we immediately express our anger or do we have the courage to stay with it for a moment?

By doing so, we might also create a new opportunity to choose our own reaction to these experiences and how we interact with our environment.

From a scientific perspective, mindfulness has been boiled down to the specific role of attention and awareness in the perception of our present moment. However, do not confuse the simplicity of this definition with the difficulty of integrating it into everyday life. Once you start the journey toward becoming more aware of all the stuff you project onto events, experiences or relationships, you quickly realize how much work is required to put it into action. Also, the Eastern origins of mindfulness are much richer. For example, becoming aware of things that are going on is just one part of the story; compassionately acting on these insights opens an entire new world of possibilities.

So bear in mind that my idea of Entrepreneurial Mindfulness goes beyond present moment awareness and attention. Nevertheless, scientific definitions allow for measurement of the current state of mindfulness of individuals as well as the effect of interventions and practice. The scales that were developed to investigate the impact of mindfulness further improved opportunities for academic research. One of the most common instruments for measuring mindfulness as a trait was developed by Kirk Brown and Richard Ryan, too.[6] The statements in this scale are intended to reflect how mindful individuals stay in everyday situations. The "Mindful Attention Awareness Scale" (MAAS) covers 15 questions that address emotional awareness, mindful eating and listening, mindful goal pursuit, and so on. As I will frequently refer to the MAAS, I highly recommend you to do a self-assessment. The scale is publicly available, but reprinting it in this book is another topic. To do the assessment, you rate the statements according to what reflects your experience rather than what you think your experience should be on a six-point scale (1-6) from "almost always" to "almost never". The scores are added and divided by 15. The higher your score, the more mindful you are as an individual! Well, from a scientific standpoint. For example, a group of Zen practitioners in Brown and Ryan's initial study averaged a score of 4.29. I will share quite a bit about my own scores in the next chapter.

Now, let's clarify the relationship between meditation and mindfulness. The good news is that a "mindfulness score" is not set in stone. For example, a study conducted by Shauna Shapiro and colleagues shows that distinct meditation-based interventions, such as MBSR, can effectively increase mindfulness as measured by the MAAS and can also have positive effects on well-being.[7] I could go on and on thinking, writing and reflecting about mindfulness. However, one of the most important things to consider is that meditation cannot really be grasped by thinking about it. Fundamentally, it is about turning your attention to the present moment, letting your thoughts come to rest, observing them and getting into a state of being. It has to be *experienced*. I completed an eight-week MBSR training in order to share first-hand experiences in the next chapter. In summary, we saw that meditation helps us to cultivate mindfulness, and a receptive attention to and awareness of present events and experiences. This in turn can have a multitude of positive effects. So, how might mindfulness relate to the specific context of entrepreneurship?

## Mindfulness and Entrepreneurial Behavior

From Part Two, you should be familiar with the concept of an entrepreneurial mindset and the theory of planned behavior. In short, the theory of planned behavior assumes that intentions are a good predictor of behavior before it can actually be observed. As discussed, the theory has been applied in various empirical studies in the context of entrepreneurship and I believe that it is an effective tool to understand the hearts and minds of entrepreneurs.

Of course, not all intentions are translated into actual behavior. Sometimes life has other plans for us... Researchers speak of an *intention-behavior gap*. Curiously, mindfulness has been included as a variable in studies on this intention-behavior relationship. Nikos Chatzisarantis and Martin Hagger applied the MAAS to study whether intentions in the context of *physical activities* and *binge-drinking* actually result in subsequent behavior.[8] They conclude that more mindful individuals are more likely to turn their intentions into actual behavior. The researchers suggest that one way that a mindful mindset helps individuals to follow their intentions is by strengthening their capacity for self-control. The authors define self-control as the ability to stay focused on the fulfillment of plans and control non-intentional impulses. These thoughts often draw people away from actually acting on their intentions. However, this is a more general study on the link between mindfulness and the intention-behavior relationship. Entrepreneurship is characterized by a very distinct context and research into mindfulness in entrepreneurial behavior is in the early stages. The same goes for the effects of meditation practice in the entrepreneurial context. Nonetheless, some interesting research is available. The first study I want to briefly introduce was published in 2019 by Marco van Gelderen and colleagues.[9] Based on two survey waves of 2092 entrepreneurs and non-entrepreneurs in Sweden, they found that individuals scoring higher in mindfulness are less likely to engage in entrepreneurial action than less mindful individuals. In the second survey wave among 450 participants who were initially non-entrepreneurs, mindful individuals started entrepreneurial action less frequently. However, when they started to act, they were as active as individuals who score low on mindfulness. Interestingly, they were even more active if they had previous entrepreneurial experience. So mindfulness might come at the cost of people thinking twice about whether starting a business is the right thing for them. This also brings us to a fundamental paradox of Entrepreneurial Mindfulness. Focusing on the future is essential for entrepreneurs. However, looking at questions 9 and 13 of the MAAS, this works directly opposite to at least, two aspects of mindfulness. These two questions refer to mindful goal pursuit and being preoccupied with the future or the past. So, there are some things we don't know yet and will probably have to find out along the way. Indeed, Marco van Gelderen and his colleagues suggest a future research agenda that investigates how Being-while-Striving might be implemented.

They also suggest that mindful individuals are more likely to perceive potentially harmful effects of their actions, so they might be more often engaged in social or sustainable entrepreneurship endeavors. This suggestion is reinforced by a 2020 study conducted by Yuval Engel and his colleagues.[10] They studied the effect of *loving-kindness meditation*

on entrepreneurs' sustainable decision-making. In their experimental studies, they found that, compared to a control group, entrepreneurs engaging in a short loving-kindness meditation experience an increase in compassion and report higher levels of sustainable decision-making. So, we can assume that including meditation practices in entrepreneurial education could result in more sustainability- or social purpose-driven ventures.

To me, this makes total sense. The more you feel connected with yourself and value the connection with others, the more you become aware of the interconnectedness of things. It is not such a bold assumption that you also start caring more about your environment. While Yuval Engel and colleagues studied the effect on entrepreneurial sustainability decision making, research has also shown broader effects of mindfulness on ethical decision making[11] and suggests several positive effects on decision making quality.[12] Consequently, we can assume that mindfulness supports entrepreneurs in making better, more ethical decisions. An assumption, which is emphasized in a Deep Dive with Yuval Engel you will find in the next part of the book.

Alright, we found arguments and research that support the first three of my propositions. However, what about entrepreneurial well-being? As I said in Part One, we need entrepreneurs to deal with the many challenges faced by human society. They need to become mindful of unfolding global events, such as climate change, social inequality and loss of biodiversity. However, Entrepreneurial Mindfulness also implies mindfulness towards the entrepreneur's own experience.

## Meditation, Mindfulness and Well-Being of Entrepreneurs

As discussed in Chapter 2, the life of entrepreneurs is often accompanied by challenges such as periods of long working hours, ambiguity and potential loneliness. Research has recently formulated agendas to help us to better understand the mechanisms and potential support for entrepreneurial well-being. At this point, it is hard to make a decisive judgement about the effect of mindfulness and meditation on entrepreneurial well-being. On the one hand, studies show plenty of positive well-being effects of mindfulness practices in the workplace. For example, studies have shown that mindfulness interventions result in reduced reported levels of burnout, perceived stress, higher resilience among managers and entrepreneurs and improved sleep quality.[13] On the other hand, scholars suggest that the context of entrepreneurship is very distinct from normal workplace settings.[14] So, research into mindfulness in the workplace is probably not directly transferable. However, the general evidence on positive effects of mindfulness-based interventions should allow us to assume that it is helpful in the entrepreneurial context, too. Additionally, some really exciting research findings are available. For example, Yuval Engel and colleagues studied the effects of loving-kindness meditation on the ability of entrepreneurs to deal with the *fear of failure*, which we discussed in Part One.[15] After following a nine-minute video exercise of loving-kindness meditation, a group of entrepreneurs showed a significantly weaker fear reaction when introduced to a failure scenario in their business than a control group. Here, self-compassion, which was improved through the meditation intervention, is the

suggested mechanism. Consequently, the authors also suggest that educators might want to introduce meditation practices into their classrooms. Interestingly, this is a recurring suggestion in several studies on the context of entrepreneurial well-being and mindfulness.[16] In order to fully understand the effects of mindfulness and meditation in the entrepreneurial context, we need testable interventions. The eight-week MBSR program provided a testable standardized approach. Maybe, the world of entrepreneurship needs something to work with, too?

Anyhow, reading about meditation will only get you so far. It is a matter of doing or rather *non-doing*. It requires intentionally taking time for *being*. That is why I would like to introduce four of my favorite meditations right away.

## Four Meditations for Entrepreneurs to Get Started

Obviously, there are hundreds of approaches to meditation, hundreds of meditation teachers and we are all different after all. I will be sharing what I learned during my own path and what works for me in my own personal practice. You can take this as a starting point for your journey. Try them for a while, for at least five minutes to experience some effects or the lack thereof. Just switching between techniques and assuming that "they are not right for you" will most likely not get you anywhere. Cultivating mindfulness can feel like hard work! However, try to approach all of them in a state of curiosity rather than expectation.

### Seated Breathing Meditation

This is probably the most simple meditation, although it is not the easiest one. Find a comfortable sitting position and stop thinking. Well... if that works for you, congratulations! For most of us, it doesn't. We get bored, frustrated, we might get confronted with some stuff that we don't really like to see or our *monkey mind* might just go nuts and shout for a *banana*! Nevertheless, I believe that a simple seated breathing meditation is the best way to intentionally do nothing and cultivate a focus on present moment experiences and events. Looking at the MAAS, aspects related to questions 3, 7, 10 or 14 might specifically benefit from such a practice.

Having found a comfortable sitting position, feel free to close your eyes, turn your attention inside and let all the thoughts, sensations and emotions be as they are. The cushion below you, sounds around you or even some tension in your neck. Take a minute of silence to appreciate where you are right now. One minute of silence is straightforward and we can all do it (yes, you too). From there, slowly turn your attention to your breath and do a little breathing exercise. Breathing is magical... Whatever crazy stuff goes on in your life, whatever goes wrong, chances are that you can still control your breath. For me, it's also a great "monkey mind banana" to calm down before more serious *non-doing*. The exercise goes like this:

- Take 5 to 10 deep inhales and exhales of 4-6 seconds into your belly
- Guide your breathe upwards and into your lower rib-cage and guide 5-10 breaths of 4-6 seconds into that area
- Turn your attention further into your upper rib-cage and guide another 5-10 breaths of 4-6 seconds to that area

- Combine all three sections (belly, lower rib-cage, upper rib-cage) and take 5-10 really deep inhales and exhales on a slow count of 6-8
- Finally, hold your breath for a second after each inhale and exhale and observe the silence during these holds

Try not to get too obsessed with the numbers and find a soothing rhythm that works for you. This exercise is all about you and not about achieving anything. If three seconds work better for you, do three seconds.

If you found your rhythm and followed it for a while, you should be quite calm now and ready to simply observe your breath for as long as you like. This is the actual meditation part. What kind of sensations can you observe in your nose? Do you feel a gentle and cooling stream of air running in and out? Try to do this for at least 5 minutes, or try 10, 20 or anything that works for you. Most importantly, do it on a regular basis. If thoughts come up, simply recognize them and let them go. Don't punish yourself for having them. That's what our minds are for. Just stay curious and take the observer's seat. You might even smile and ask yourself:

## "What might be my next thought?"

Whenever it comes up, gently return to your breath. After you are done with the formal practice, try to take this feeling of calmness and focus into whatever you do next. Everything can be your practice if you bless it with the right attitude, your full awareness and wholehearted attention.

### Loving-Kindness Meditation

As we learned from scientific studies earlier, this one

is promising for entrepreneurs. Turning your ideas into reality can be a lonely experience at times. Not everyone is blessed with a dynamic founding team right from the beginning or you might work on stuff that your teammates have no clue about. Loving-kindness meditation has its origins in Buddhist tradition; you might see it being referred to with the Sanskrit word *Metta*. Metta is also one of the essential ingredients of a good Thai massage the way I learned it from my friend and teacher Lucie. Being with someone with all your heart and attention is one of the greatest gifts you can give. But what about you? Can you be with yourself with all your heart? Do you remember the first question in the MAAS earlier? It refers to being conscious of the emotions you are experiencing.

Loving-kindness meditation is a good way to cultivate awareness of your own emotional experience. It usually runs through five stages; I recommend starting with a simple seated meditation as described before to get into the present moment. From there, focus on the area around your heart. You can even put your hands on your chest in the heart area. With your full presence and all your heart, speak the following phrases to yourself:

**"May I be well. May I be free from suffering. May I thrive on pursuing my dreams and aspirations. May I find meaningful connections within me and with the world around me. May I be happy and fulfilled. "**

The meditation is essentially about the feelings and emotions that the words evoke within you. So while you are saying them to yourself, stay centered on what they are doing for you. In the beginning it might feel odd to be saying these kinds of things to yourself, which is a good indicator that you should do it more often. Self-responsibility begins with the realization that we are indeed worthy of having all these things in our life. After you say them, keep your attention turned inside for a minute. You might also want to change the sentences or words to something that resonates with you. Repeat the words kindly, return your attention to the phrases and the feelings they evoke whenever your thoughts start wandering.  Proceeding in our loving-kindness journey, we now choose a person that we would intuitively bless with these wishes. For me, that is usually my parents, one of my sisters or my partner. Again, we speak to our self:

**"May you be well. May you be free from suffering. May you thrive on pursuing your dreams and aspirations. May you find meaningful connections within you and with the world around you. May you be happy and fulfilled. "**

From there, we proceed to a person that is neutral to us. Do you always gratefully appreciate all the people that you meet during the day as human beings? The pandemic might show many of us how precious this human connection really is. Here is the chance to bless your local coffee lady with some loving-kindness:

**"May you be well. May you be free from suffering. May you thrive on pursuing your dreams and aspirations. May you find meaningful connections within you and with the world around you. May you be happy and fulfilled. "**

Then turn our attention and heart to someone you might have a difficult relationship with. That's where the hard work begins:

"May you be well. May you be free from suffering. May you thrive on pursuing your dreams and aspirations. May you find meaningful connections within you and with the world around you. May you be happy and fulfilled. "

Finally, we include all the people above and all beings; humans, animals and whatever beings you believe to exist.

"May all beings be well. May all beings be free from suffering. May all beings thrive on pursuing their dreams and aspirations. May all beings find meaningful connections within them and with the world around them. May all beings be happy and fulfilled. "

Stay with the focus on your heart area for a little while. Try to appreciate every sensation within you and stay curious about how this meditation might have changed your emotional state. Again, the formal practice is only a beginning of bringing mindfulness and compassion into your everyday life. The real work begins when things are going wrong or unfold in unexpected ways. How do you react? Are you still able to treat yourself with compassion and refrain from giving yourself a harsh talk? This is the practice, too.

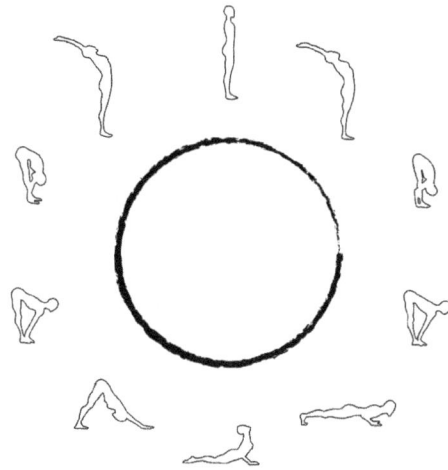

*Figure 7: A simple sun salutation (illustrated by Anna-Lena Krohn).*

I stumbled into this one when I was eleven years old, and my friend Dominik took me to my first ever Tae Kwon Do session. Martial arts, acrobatics, Yoga, dancing, you name it... They can all be a medium to meditate in motion. I remember shouting "This is meditation in motion!" in my practical Yoga teacher exam, while guiding the group through a rather challenging Vinyasa flow. Looking back, I do not think everybody felt the way I did (there were many sweaty faces and tired eyes). Well, I'm still learning.

Anyway, from my point of view, the most important ingredient is intentionality. You can do all sorts of physical activity, and they might be healthy and they might get you into a flow state, but I would argue that not all of them allow you to meditate in motion. Yoga (the Asana part, that is) works well because it has a decent level of complexity and is usually performed rather slowly. It provides fertile ground for exploring your body through stretching and strengthening exercises. Most Yoga session also include meditations and the body scan, which we will have a look at shortly. However, without intentionally directing your attention to the experience of every movement and its effects, Yoga can also become a physical exercise like any other. A simple sun salutation is a great exercise to move the body in various directions; it can be done in just a couple of minutes. I agree with Jon Kabat-Zinn in recommending you take some time for this every day[17], even if it is just one mindful sun salutation:

1. Start in an upright position and ground your two feet on the floor
   a. Make sure your weight is evenly balanced on your entire feet, engage your legs slightly, pull your knee caps up and relax your shoulders
   b. Take a moment to feel the stability of this proud, strong *mountain pose*
2. Inhale, lift your arms to the side and, if it feels right for you, come into a gentle backbend
3. Exhale and slowly come into a forward fold
   a. Bend your legs as much as you like and simply let your hands arrive wherever they arrive — this exercise is really not about touching the floor, your feet or anything else in particular
   b. Simply let gravity do the work and bend your back, relax your arms, shoulders and neck
4. Inhale, gaze forward without putting too much tension on your neck and straighten your back
5. Exhale, walk your feet back until you are in a planche position and slowly lower your body to the floor
6. While you are still exhaling, press into your hands and come into a backbend
   a. Squeeze your glutes and slightly activate your core to prevent your lower back from getting compressed (if you know what a posterior pelvic tilt is, that is what you want)
   b. Do not collapse into your shoulders (pull shoulder blades together and down)
7. Inhale, flip your feet, come into a downward facing dog and stay there for 3-5 breaths
   a. Bend your knees as much as you need
   b. Keep a straight line from your sacrum to your wrists
   c. Work your heels towards the floor, if you can keep your back straight
8. With your next inhale, walk your feet towards your hands and come into an active forward fold
9. Exhale and come into a passive forward fold
10. Inhale, role your back up vertebra by vertebra, lift your arms up and arrive in a gentle backbend if it feels right for you
    a. You can do this really slow and cultivate awareness for your spine

11. Exhale and return to your mountain pose

A sun salutation is a wonderful sequence of movements that includes gentle stretches, some strengthening exercises and allows to connect your movements with your breath. I cannot even write about it without doing one.

## Body Scan

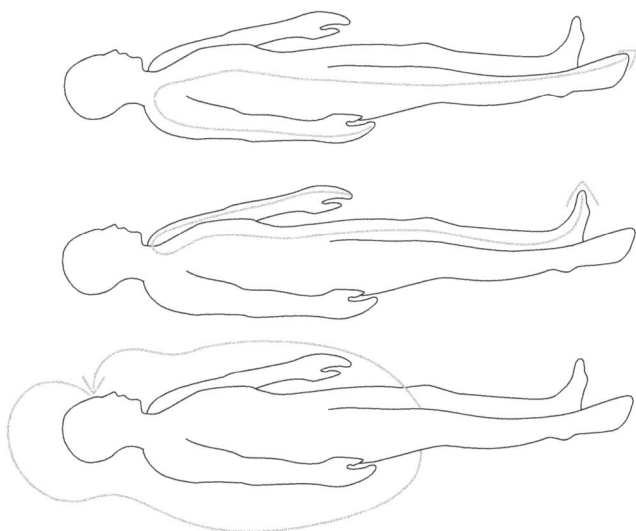

*Figure 8: Three phases of a body scan (illustrated by Anna-Lena Krohn).*

Finally, and this is an amazing one after meditating in motion, there is the body scan. Another question from the scale we discussed earlier refers to noticing feelings of physical discomfort. Intentionally taking time to feel your own body, to create a connection with this absolutely amazing gift that we all have is so precious. We have a tendency to direct our attention to the sensations that shout the loudest, but there is usually so much more going on. Lie down on the floor, grab a blanket to make sure that it is warm enough and ensure you will not get disturbed for a couple of minutes. Take your own minute of silence. Now, let me take you on a journey through your body.

Starting with your right hand, guide your attention through your fingers starting with your right thumb. What are the subtle sensations that you can get aware of by focusing your attention on that specific part of your body? Is it warm? Is it vibrating? Is there no sensation at all? Stay for a couple of seconds before you proceed. Everything is welcome and there is no right or wrong. The time you are taking and the will to explore your present moment experience is all that you need. With the same attitude of curiosity, make your way through the four other fingers, your palm, the back of your hands, your wrist, your lower arm, your upper arm, your shoulder and the side of your body. How deep can you go? Can you feel other structures than your skin? Your muscles, bones or ligaments? Spend some time at every part of your body and do not rush through it. Enjoy the process and try not to turn this into another to-do on your list. If you drift away in daydreams, shopping lists or thoughts about your crush, give yourself a smile and come back to your body scan. If you become aware of your mind wandering, congratulations; this is a moment of pure mindfulness. From the side of your body, guide your attention through the hips, your upper leg, your knee and knee cap, your lower leg, your ankle and finally your feet and toes. Take a moment to sense the awareness you created in the entire right side of your body. Repeat the journey on your body's left side, taking a moment to feel it, and then focus your attention on both sides of the body for a while. Finally, start the process for your torso in the area between your eyes. Guide your attention through the highest point of your head, your neck, your spine and the muscles next to it, your sacrum, your buttocks and the groin area. Move towards the abdomen and chest area. Again, try to sense deeper areas of your body. Can you feel your organs? Can you feel how your breath affects your diaphragm, ribcage and lungs? Slowly and steadily guide your attention to the throat, jaw, lips, teeth, tongue, nose and eyes. Then, open your awareness to all your sensations in the torso and finally to your entire body. Stay here for a while and enjoy the awareness and alertness you have created for all your body sensations.

## In a Nutshell...

I hope the exercises in this chapter gave you an idea of how meditation can be used to cultivate mindfulness and other mental qualities such as compassion. Entrepreneurs matter, their purpose matters and it matters how they act on their goals. What if mindfulness and meditation practice would support society in empowering changemakers to start and realize ventures, which are guided by socially- and sustainability-driven purposes? What if it helped entrepreneurs to do so more effectively, more sustainably and with less negative experiences related to their social, physical or mental well-being?

Nevertheless, fully resolving the apparent paradox of Being-while-Striving is still up for discussion. In the next part of the book, I will take some chances and start envisioning how we might approach creating the future from the present moment. However, before we can talk about the creative part of "making Entrepreneurial Mindfulness a thing", an important piece is missing: the eight-week MBSR self-experiment. I have stressed several times that mindfulness needs to be experienced and, of course, I will walk the talk. In the next chapter, you will read about my own experience of becoming more mindful in times of creating the future. But what about you? The good news is, if you did all four exercises of this chapter, you just completed your first Yoga session. Usually, it involves a period of meditation in the beginning, setting an intention for the practice, like cultivating loving-kindness towards yourself, a good deal of movement practice (Asana) and a lying meditation (Shavasana). Maybe you have got a slightly better idea of why these practices make sense and how they help you to get more mindful in everyday life. Yet, looking at the MAAS, there are many more things that need to be cultivated: Eating mindfully, communicating mindfully and walking mindfully. Nevertheless, formal practice is essential for truly experiencing what the space between stimulus and response feels like and consequently taking this wisdom into your everyday life. Meditation is not something that you figure out by thinking about it. You need to practice it! Take time for non-doing and turn your attention inward to become aware of all the funky stuff that's going on. Today, I would like you to formulate an implementation intention that gives you a realistic chance of turning meditation into a habit over the next 30 days. I committed to meditating for an hour every day for the eight weeks of my MBSR course. How much can you do? Maybe 5, 10, or 20 minutes?

# I Dare You:

## Plan a Formal Meditation Practice!

- Try the four meditations in this chapter and choose the one that resonates with you the most, to begin with
- When I asked you how much you want to commit, which number popped up in your head? Take that and add another 5 minutes, at least. Seriously, you want to get out of your comfort zone
- For me, meditation usually begins after 10-15 minutes. That is when my body seems to calm down and my mind seems to accept the non-doing mode
- Think a moment about the time that would work for you. I like to do it in the early mornings, but we are all unique human beings. Choose a time that works for you and that might help you to recharge
- Take a piece of paper and draw 30 boxes and the according dates for each box
- Guess what's next... Do it! Tick the boxes. Even if you don't feel like it one day, do it. This is the practice. We are only talking about 30 days after all...
  - Remember the implementation intention thing from Part Two? Here is your chance to try it out!
- Just see what happens; you can still decide that meditation is nothing for you. But I would be surprised if you do!
- Ideally, start a diary to reflect on your experiences and how they might slowly find their way into dealing with everyday challenges

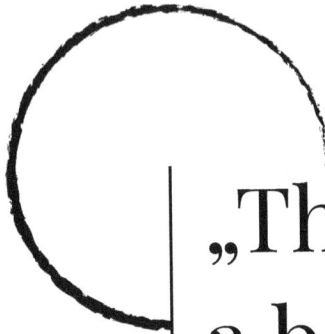

„The Mind:
a beautiful servant,
a dangerous
master."

OSHO

# 06 An Entrepreneurial Mindfulness Self-Experiment

Recently, I have been busy doing nothing. Well, not really. I was busy trying to figure out what the idea of Being-while-Striving feels like in real life... In Chapter 5, I indicated that, if Entrepreneurial Mindfulness is to become a thing, we need to understand how to approach this apparent paradox. Entrepreneurs act on opportunities to create something that does not exist yet. By definition, they engage in goal-directed behavior and strive for the outcome of their actions. Obviously, they rely on their mind to do a lot of thinking for them. I recall that mindfulness, however, is about a non-judgmental focus on the *present moment*.[18] Additionally, Jon Kabat-Zinn describes non-striving as one of the pillars of mindfulness practice in his book *Full Catastrophe Living*.[19] With regard to the opening quote from Osho, how do entrepreneurs make sure they stay on top of things and that they don't get lost in their own thought? You might be starting to get an idea as to why pure logic might not resolve this question.

## Being-While-Striving

Originally proposed by Marco van Gelderen and his colleagues, the idea of Being-while-Striving is fundamental to understanding the interplay of mindfulness and entrepreneurship.[20] However, they suggested it as a topic for future research and did not investigate the idea itself. Since their article was published as recently as 2019, we cannot expect to get a scientific answer to this question very soon. Nevertheless, we can have a closer look at the individual concepts of *being* and *striving*. Furthermore, scholars who explore mindfulness in other workplace settings have discovered a similar phenomenon. Christopher Lyddy and Darren Good published a study in 2017 which investigates the potential paradox of *Being-while-Doing*.[21] What can entrepreneurs learn from mindfulness in the workplace? Additionally, I will complement these insights with my own experiences. How did I personally experience the challenge of Being-while-Striving?

Let's begin with the *being* part of things. What is it and why might it conflict with modes of *doing* or even *striving*? In their study of exploring the idea of Being-while-Doing, Christopher Lyddy and Darren Good conceptualize a mode of *being* as characterized by aspects, like:

- A temporal focus on the present moment
- Non-conceptual perception
- A non-judgmental attitude
- Being self-quieted
- A goalless orientation and intentional behavior

If you ever joined a guided meditation or even a mindfulness program, you will recognize many of these elements as common cues in such practices. Fundamentally, meditation is about intentionally getting into a state of *being* or mindfulness. If you are not an experienced meditator, you might recognize moments of *being* from other situations. Examples might include being close to nature, close to people that are important to you or even small rituals that you do for the sake of doing them. I am not a particularly good surfer, but sitting in the ocean, watching the waves and occasionally taking my chance on riding one of them gets me into such a mode. So, what might be the issue with regard to workplace or even entrepreneurial settings? According to Lyddy and Good, workplace settings are typically characterized by a mode of *doing* or goal-directed cognition. Here, we get the first hint of an entrepreneurial context. As we saw in Chapters 3 and 4, the entrepreneurial journey is inherently goal-directed and it relies heavily on envisioning the outcome of acting on opportunities. The *doing* mode is further characterized by aspects, like:

- A temporal focus on past and future
- Conceptual perception
- A judgmental attitude
- Being self-centered
- A goal-directed orientation and automatic behavior

In that sense, entrepreneurship is an extreme form of *doing* or, as implied by Marco van Gelderen and colleagues, a mode of *striving*.[22] Indeed, entrepreneurs have to be strongly focused on the future, opportunities that entrepreneurs act on are fundamentally conceptual connections between means and anticipated outcomes. Pretty much every startup has a founding narrative that it proudly communicates, and getting a viable business running requires a constant judgment of potential paths of action. Often, these judgments have to be made so quickly and frequently that automatic agency is probably not a bad way of putting it. Furthermore, looking back at the Deep Dive with Rogelio, the entrepreneurial journey can be considered a marathon than a sprint. From my point of view, *mindful striving* might be even trickier to implement than *mindful doing*.

Before Lyddy and Good approached the question with an empirical investigation, and talked to people who engage in the struggle to stay mindful at work, the relationship between *being* and *doing* was defined as being anything between antithetical and complementary. An antithetical view points out that a mode of *being* might be inversely related to a mode of *doing*, because mindfulness may correspond with reduced activation in brain regions associated with important aspects of *doing*. Contrary to that view, Darren Good and colleagues found in an earlier study that mindfulness has an array of positive effects on workplace functioning and might be complementary with a mode of *doing*.

Lyddy and Good had conversations with 39 people who try to approach their work more mindfully. Many interviewees shared experiences of staying mindful while working or Being-while-Doing. Furthermore, many participants reported that they were usually feeling and functioning better when they managed to stay mentally quiet, remain present, refrained from constant judgement and maintained other qualities typical of a state of mindfulness while doing their work. An important thing here is that people were still doing their work or thinking and contemplating the future, *while* staying aware of the present moment. Of course, ideally, individuals would constantly stay in such a synergetic mode. However, participants also shared many experiences of struggling to stay mindful at work. While it seems possible, it is a big practical challenge and several people reported unintentionally being pulled into and then getting lost in their mental worlds. Other words the interviewees used were "lost in thought", "carried away" or "enmeshed". Does that rings a bell?

As previously shown in many studies of mindfulness at work, people reported positive effects of staying mindful and negative effects of getting entangled in a pure mode of *doing*. Therefore, properties activated by a mode of *being* may act as a resource that enables alternative psychological processes. By contrast, a pure doing mode might have negative implications. Finally, the model of Being-while-Doing also presents some potential important antecedents to staying mindful at work. Of course, some jobs are inherently more challenging and situational aspects like a challenging work situation could draw our attention away from the present moment. Therefore, we can assume that entrepreneurs are generally more challenged than, for example, a librarian. Interestingly, people are frequently drawn into becoming less mindful by *emotional triggers*. We will talk more about the role of emotions and how meditation helps to handle them in the next chapter. However, situational factors like a calm private space can support individuals' ability to stay mindful. Not surprisingly, *recency*, *frequency* and *cumulative lifetime* practice of meditation play another important role in being able to stay mindful at work. Furthermore, participants shared different levels of perceived self-efficacy when it comes to returning to a mode of *being* in challenging work situations. Hence, it is also a very individual challenge.

In summary, Lyddy and Good showed that a hybrid mode of Being-while-Doing is indeed possible. This bears huge potential for better workplace functioning and well-being. However, constantly staying in this mode seems to be a tough challenge which requires dedicated practice and which partially depends on external factors. One such factor is the type of work that requires the *doing* mode. From my point of view, entrepreneurship is a challenging environment indeed and one that even requires a mode of *striving*. Yet, there is no reason to assume that attaining a mode of Being-while-Striving is impossible.

So much for the theory. Let's get to the experiential part of things. Before I reflect my own experience, I quickly want to share some thoughts on why this experience might help to shed some light on the "black box" of Being-while-Striving.

## Crossing the Entrepreneurial Rubicon

I believe that two questions need to be considered to make a judgment here. First, am I an entrepreneur? Well, personally, I would clearly say yes. I am on a mission to empower changemakers and I am striving to "make Entrepreneurial Mindfulness a thing". However, you might already be used to my mostly scientific approach to things. In Chapter 3, I introduced the entrepreneurial journey and the idea of an *entrepreneurial Rubicon*: a specific point at which a *nascent entrepreneur* shows enough entrepreneurial action to be considered a *new entrepreneur*.[23] Marco van Gelderen and colleagues present 12 so called gestation actions to make this assessment in a study about mindfulness and its effect on entrepreneurial action.[24] In their study, no participant reported more than seven of these activities, which consequently marked their maximum point of early entrepreneurial activity. Prior to starting my MBSR training, I conducted the following gestation actions, which Marco van Gelderen and colleagues list:

- Developing a product or service (e.g. I was working on this book)

85

- Conducting market research (e.g. talking to people like Rogelio and understanding their entrepreneurial needs)
- Discussing a product or service with potential customers (e.g. my conversation with Yuval Engel in Chapter 7)
- Creating a homepage (www.onmindsandmotion.com)
- Making a cooperation agreement with another business (e.g. with the University of Twente in Chapter 9)
- Hiring an employee or intern (my sister supported me with layout and typeset of this book)
- Acquiring resources (e.g. an Adobe Creative Cloud license)

I count seven actions. Here we go, science says I am an entrepreneur! However, the other important question is "am I doing so in a mindful way?" Spoiler alert! Without saying too much about the actual experiment, I certainly try to do so, but it is a challenge. I practiced mindful approaches to movement, such as martial arts and Yoga, for almost two decades. Furthermore, during recent years I incorporated more and more formal meditation practices into my routines. Nevertheless, I had no dedicated daily meditation practice, so I felt like joining an MBSR program should be a good starting point.

To add a little bit more context, during the period of the experiment I was collecting the data for my on-going PhD, was part of the management team for a MSc. program and I was pushing my entrepreneurial vision. Frankly speaking, it was a damn stressful time and I needed more effective tools to handle the soaring effects of that stress while staying productive. Also, I simply enjoy life and realized that all my *striving* slowly creeped into my personal life and my capacity for "being in the moment". I needed support to "get out of my mind".

Let me share what I experienced during my MBSR program, which was guided by Hanna Tempelhagen of The Mindful Spaces, Hamburg. We touched on the MBSR program in Chapter 5. In short, it involves guided weekly sessions of meditation, reflection and group discussions. We will now go into some more details to lay ground for the actual self-experiment journal, a Deep Dive with myself.

## The Mindfulness Based Stress Reduction Program

Since Jon Kabat-Zinn developed the MBSR program and published first study results in 1982, research on mindfulness and its effects has taken off.[25] While the Eastern roots of mindfulness, meditation and spiritual practices date back thousands of years, they are rich, complex and diverse. I personally see a lot of beauty in this diversity and it potentially takes lifetimes to explore all the facets of these practices. But it doesn't particularly simplify a scientist's job to measure and test the effects of interventions. Hence, Jon Kabat-Zinn did an important service to the scientific community by providing something to begin with, that is complex enough to reflect the richness of Eastern traditions and simple enough to be accessible to researchers and participants in the Western world. We know that it works, but scholars are still untangling which components of the program lead to which effects.[26] Here, I will share the approach of The Mindful Spaces.

## MBSR General Structure and Setting

MBSR trainings are carried out in a group setting. Each week entails a 120 to 150 minute session with guided meditation practice, exercises of incorporating mindfulness into everyday life and group reflections. We were a group of twelve and our teacher Hanna usually did the full 150 minutes. For example, we did a widely known mindfulness exercise in which participants explore a raisin with all their senses — seeing, feeling, hearing (I had to squeeze it a little), smelling and tasting — before eating it mindfully and slowly. Besides the weekly sessions, there is also a day of silence and participants commit to a daily guided meditation practice of 40 to 60 minutes. Lastly, the group also celebrates a full day of silence.

## MBSR Formal Meditation Practices

The formal meditation practices of our MBSR course covered sitting meditation, body scan and mindful movement. Furthermore, on the day of silence we explored several other practices, such as walking meditation and loving-kindness meditation. As a little recap, sitting meditation works with awareness of body sensations, thoughts, emotions and/or continually returning the focus of attention to the breath or other *mental anchors*. The body scan progressively moves attention through the body from toes to head while observing sensations in all regions of the body. Mindful movement refers to Hatha-Yoga inspired stretches and postures. These so-called *Asanas* are designed to enhance awareness of the body. Furthermore, they balance and strengthen the musculoskeletal system. Lastly, the loving-kindness meditation is intended to develop greater compassion for oneself, others, and

humanity in a wider sense. In all practices, participants are asked to bring their attention to the present moment, in order to cultivate mindfulness.

## Synthesis and Qualities of Mindfulness

Finally, besides the general setting and formal practice, certain topics are covered during the weekly sessions and integrated into reflective discussions. In the case of my training, the integration of mindfulness in everyday life was facilitated in the following way:

- Week 1 — Unlocking the inner resources
- Week 2 — Exploring how we perceive the world
- Week 3 — Feeling at home in our body
- Week 4 — Consciously turning our attention to stress
- Week 5 – Discovering our freedom to choose how to respond to stress
- Week 6 — Learning to communicate mindfully
- Week 7 — Becoming familiar with self-care
- Week 8 — How to individually sustain a mindfulness and meditation practice

These topics, in combination with formal and informal topics, lead to cultivation of certain inner qualities — one of them obviously being mindfulness. But there are other elements that contribute to living more mindfully and seeing the things as they really are. The handbook of my MBSR training lists the following attitudes:

- Self-responsibility
- Non-judgment
- Patience
- Beginner's mind

- Trust
- Non-striving
- Acceptance
- Letting go

If you are interested in more details, you will find them in Kabat-Zinn's book, *Full Catastrophe Liv-* *ing.*[27] Furthermore, I complemented the training with weekly journaling exercises, daily reflection on mindfulness using the Mindful Awareness Attention Scale[28] and biweekly reflection of my well-being using the WHO-5 Well-Being Scale.[29] Let's begin the Deep Dive with myself!

# Deep Dive

A Conversation with Myself,
the Aspiring Mindful Entrepreneur

## My Weekly Journal

Every Sunday evening, I took some time to reflect on the formal as well as informal impulses for practice and how they affected me and my *striving*. Our weekly sessions took place on Tuesday. So, I decided to start the Sunday before the actual training.

### Week 0 — Sunday, October 18th 2020

Malte: Well, the last two weeks have been kind of a ride... I started the data collection for my PhD thesis a while ago and this got me into worrying about its outcome quite a bit. I worked three years to get to this point and not being able to get the data I need would really be a bummer. Besides that, our new cohort of innovation management master's students is starting tomorrow. I will teach a course on *empathic communication* and how it supports efforts to drive change. I am looking forward to it, but it also requires my full presence, and it will be the first lecture I have delivered all by myself. All the while, I keep on writing for *The Mindful Startup*. This is an important step to create traction for the ideas behind Entrepreneurial Mindfulness and, consequently, to establish awareness of these ideas. Strategically, I believe that I will need this book to turn my mission into a viable venture. I am passionate about all these projects, but they require discipline, time management and a lot of *thinking*. It is a challenge to stay as present as I possibly can in my relationship, enjoy the little everyday things and keep up my physical practice. I feel like I am dancing at the edge of my capacity, if you want to put it that way. It even got to the point that I am not sleeping well, which I personally consider a red flag for my well-being. October and November will most likely stay like that and I hope that the training will mindfully get me towards a more balanced end of the year.

### Week 1 — Sunday, October 25th 2020

Malte: This week, we kicked off the new cohort of innovation management students with an intense induction week and I held my first lecture, which dealt with *empathic communication* as a key soft skill for changemakers. I enjoyed teaching the lecture, but being continuously present and available to the students was quite a mental challenge. The beginning of the MBSR course was well-timed and gave me a great environment to refocus. It started at 7:30 pm and went on until 10:00 pm. Honestly, it was tough not to fall asleep during the body scan, which is our main meditation for this week. So far, I did it every morning. I have done body scans before, but never for 45 minutes, which feels pretty long. My mind starts wandering all the time. Also, today, for the first time, I got a bit annoyed by the repetitiveness... I guess that's part of the experience. I cannot say that I generally feel "more mindful", yet. However, as part of our homework, I ate a very slow and mindful meal on Friday and that was a truly joyful experience! I will try to do that more often. I am also trying to stick to my writing schedule, which is a challenge. This weekend, I had to do some more self-care and did not manage to write as much as I would like to. Generally speaking, all my *striving* gets me into my head quite a lot. So, this experiment might get interesting...

### Week 2 — Sunday, November 1ˢᵗ 2020

Malte: The last two weeks have been less challenging. Maybe I also became better at handling it. Successfully delivering my lecture during the induction week was fun and a big milestone for this year. I managed to schedule two more interviews for my book and should be able to cover most of the topics I want to finish this year. Also, I created a document draft of the book and it looks promising. I believe that it will create a great foundation to take things with my entrepreneurial mission forward. Credibility is probably a good way to put it. Still, I don't really know what I am getting myself into and my head occasionally gets caught up in worrying about that. The MBSR course seems to be slowly changing things. Our formal practice is still mainly the body scan and we added a self-guided 10-minute breathing meditation. Overall, my meditation practice is getting a bit deeper and more focused. Pushing through the repetitiveness, letting go of expectations and sinking into my own body seems to do something for me. Our informal task for the week was to look out for the joys of everyday life. That is something I try to do on a regular basis anyway, but I feel that I enjoyed it a little bit more. Maybe, my mode of *being* kicks in here? I observed the warmth of the autumn sun in the morning, a dog playfully chasing some oak leaves, a dynamic team of students acing their challenges, a bright red maple tree, and a joyful crowd of Yogis and Yoginis celebrating the last practice before the Corona lockdown together. Small things that make life worth living and often get lost in stressful times and striving for the future. Being-while-Striving... Let's see if I can fully get there. Certainly only by being fully here.

### Week 3 — Sunday, November 8ᵗʰ 2020

Malte: This week was kind of average in most regards. We now alternate guided body scans with a guided 45-minute Yoga practice and do a 15-minute daily breathing meditation. Since I have practiced Yoga for many years, the meditation practice was mostly easy to maintain (with some ups, downs and occasional body scan naps, of course). Interestingly, my breathing meditations seem to get deeper again with some more intense sensations. I had kind of lost that in the last months and I am curious if these experiences will be more regular again. I am beginning to understand why this highly structured approach to MBSR seems to do the job for many people. Generally, I seem to get more relaxed, but I am far from where I was during my Yoga teacher training. Besides that, I get kind of bored by the routines that guide my everyday life. But hey... We are in the middle of a pandemic. The highlight of my week with regard to well-being were the nice walks with my girlfriend. Also, my workload was OK and the *striving* part of things was less intense.

### Week 4 — Sunday, November 15ᵗʰ 2020

Malte: Our formal practice mainly remained the same, with the breathing meditation now lasting 20 minutes. However, this week I feel like I am getting calmer and I contemplate my emotional reactions to things a lot. In the last MBSR session we talked about stress triggers and our internal responses. I personally figured out that I get stressed when I worry about things that might go wrong in the future or are out of my control.

Maybe that is an inherent risk of *striving*? However, when things do get out of hand, I am usually quite calm, rational and I act swiftly. I also have no issues with doing a late shift to get important stuff done or saying no when I can't handle things. It's funny, because I often worry that I started too many tasks and rarely have to do the actual night shift. My time management works really well. I figured out that I need more trust in myself. Buddhists speak of a *trusting heart* and it seems that this should be part of my personal practice. Of course, actually maintaining a *trusting heart* in the situations that trigger me will be a journey beyond the MBSR course. Nevertheless, becoming aware of such things is obviously the first step of this journey. Additionally, I got to know about Paul Gilbert's *three systems model of affect regulation* and I found it very helpful for reflection. So, I integrated it to this week's writing and discussed it with my teacher Hanna Tempelhagen for another Deep Dive. On the more entrepreneurial side of things, "making Entrepreneurial Mindfulness a thing" got accepted as a project by the University of Stanford's d.school and this is exciting! It might create traction for getting the idea out there and increasing the likelihood that I can build a viable venture around empowering changemakers. This might also be complemented by an upcoming opportunity to offer a course or training concept at a university. Indeed, I have not stopped striving to make Entrepreneurial Mindfulness a thing. However, I am beginning to do so more mindfully. I am slowly getting better at identifying the tiny moments in which I have the freedom of not getting completely entangled in my *striving*.

## Week 5 — Sunday, November 22nd 2020

Malte: We now alternate Yoga, body scan and a 45-minute guided seated meditation. 45 minutes of sitting and intentionally doing nothing... It is tough! Yet, last week was interesting in two regards. I had a highly interesting meditation experience. Somehow, I was so calm that I felt how my thoughts emerged and in some instances was able to let them go before they got to my consciousness. In that regard, I would describe it as an experience of pure mindfulness. I became aware of the internal event of an emerging thought and intentionally turned my attention back to my breath. This came along with a realization. My meditations were much deeper and fulfilling during and after the Yoga teacher training in 2019. However, I was in an environment that did not require me to *think* and *do* as much as I do now. There's simply not as much to think about in a retreat space in Bali. Hence, the challenge truly will be to manage Being-while-Striving: to balance them and create the future from the present moment without constantly getting entirely absorbed in it. It is challenging and it will remain so. But I still believe it is the right way for me and it will be worthwhile to keep up the meditation practice. However, during the course, I have also realized how much my movement practice allows me to feel connected to myself. This in turn allows me to deal with emotions that come up during challenging life situations better. This is something I struggled with during the week, because I do not move as much as I would like to. We all get the same 24 hours a day. Taking an hour for meditation from a full day and an entire evening for the weekly MBSR sessions obviously implies compromises. In the long run, I will have to find a balance between formal meditation and my movement practice. Today, I ran for 10 kilometers, went out to move and did handstands for two hours. The *trusting heart* is back. I understand why MBSR works and I believe the formalized structure is a great start. Yet, it is only the beginning of another journey. *Self-responsibility* then requires us to find our own personal balance and practice. Also, most of us do not live in a Yoga retreat space. We have to find our own individual way of Being-while-Striving. Personally, I am passionate about the thing I am *striving* for. How I am going to advocate Entrepreneurial Mindfulness? I still don't know. But I am currently experiencing its potential and I know that I will find ways to scale the idea. That is a question of product development, business model design and understanding customer journeys: all things that I study, research and teach. Why would I not have a *trusting heart* and the confidence to pull this off?

### Week 6 — Sunday, November 29th 2020

Malte: Today, I spent the day in silence during our MBSR day of mindfulness, which is quite a nice way to start my 33rd year on this planet (yesterday was my birthday). The day was filled with five hours of meditation practice. Seated, walking, body scan, loving-kindness, you name it! While the sitting part became physically challenging at times, I enjoyed the internal practice most of the time. I haven't felt as calm as I do right now for a long while. I also believe that I am becoming more and more aware of the mechanisms that trigger stress responses and it is becoming more and more natural to integrate meditations into my daily routines. Sometimes, mindful moments also arrive unintentionally when I hold my coffee, when I go for a walk or when I spend time with the fellow humans I love. Besides that, I finished some important tasks, such as collecting the necessary data for my dissertation project. That being said, I believe that there are limits to how much I can engage in *thinking* and still being able to really get "out of my mind". I still believe that we can get into a mode of Being-while-Striving and that cultivating mindfulness is of great value for entrepreneurs and innovators. However, appreciating one's own capacity also means to learn when to take time for pure *being*.

Meditating is not simply something you put on top of a busy day and there you are. Being a mindful entrepreneur also means becoming aware of your own capacity. Sure, getting out of our comfort zone provides room for growth. Step out of it too much and you might sacrifice things in an irreversible way. Stress can have serious effects on our physical and mental health. On a more subtle side, our relationships might suffer even more silently. I am blessed with a very sensitive partner who is not shy about telling me when my attention is not 100% with her. And to be honest, this happens at times when I dwell on the complex interaction of ideas behind this book. Meditation helps, but there are limits and I remember my Deep Dive with Dagmar, who said that entrepreneurs should not get lost in their cause too much. Yes, we can create the future from the present moment and yes, meditation helps with that. But life is so much richer, and living it to the fullest is still the best way that I know to stay grounded in the present moment. Often, it happens outside of the entrepreneurial act!

### Week 7- Sunday, December 6th 2020

Malte: Moments in which I feel at peace and dwell on the present moment are occurring more and more frequently. Or should I say that I become aware of them more frequently? Enjoying a piece of chocolate, feeling the warmth of a cup of tea and sensing the warm light of a candle while the world outside gets darker and slows down. Of course, I can't tell if this is the result of me meeting some important milestones, like the data collection for my PhD. However, I still get into challenging situations and I continue to challenge myself. I am still *striving*. For example, I just submitted a proposal for a class about Entrepreneurial Mindfulness. If it gets accepted, I will have to create the content, plan the sessions and carry them out while writing my PhD thesis. Yet, I feel confident that it would all work out. Overall, the MBSR training has provided me with some effective tools to clearly identify the moments when I get out of my Being-while-Striving mode. In my opinion, a crucial part of this is taking time for formal meditation: time to clearly let the *striving* mode come to a rest and create an awareness for the mental space, which is so crucial for staying present in challenging situations. Osho is really on to something when he says that the mind is a beautiful servant but a dangerous master. I am now experiencing first-hand the fact that indeed, the mind can be tamed while being challenged. However, I still think there are limits. Meditation and mindfulness can surely help. But, as I said, it is not something you can just put on top of a busy day and expect it to fix everything. It does not replace a need for self-responsibility and conscious decisions about how much we can compromise on times of *being*. We all get the same 24 hours a day, and creating the future from the present moment will require certain sacrifices on the *striving* side in exchange for the ability to stay present. Being-while-Striving might be possible, but it is also a matter of finding the right balance between these modes.

## Week 8 — Sunday, December 13th 2020

Malte: The MBSR training is over and I had some time to get into my own practice for a while. Looking back to eight weeks ago, I definitely see significant changes. Generally speaking, I am much more calm and, if something stressful comes up, I am able to find that space in between stimulus and reaction much better. It is still not easy and I am not saying that I will always be able to stay "Zen", but I have a reference point now. I do not just understand the idea of bringing mindfulness into these situations, I have also experienced it. I also experienced the fact that the loving, kind version of me needs this balance and calmness. Since it is the person I want to be, I know what to do now. Actually, there is a good example for this. I had a difficult conversation with my partner this week, which kind of evoked some of my old "emotional demons". However, I was able to listen to her points, and I tried to understand her perspective before sharing what was going on within me. It was an interesting experience because there was space for all the things that I felt, but they did not guide my actions. Similarly, I believe that this is so valuable in dealing with the difficulties of driving change. Finding a healthy way of dealing with the emotional journey of uncertainty, ambiguity and looming failure still seems promising to me. Now, I can say that a structured and guided mindfulness based training is an effective method for doing so. Beside my personal challenges, I am currently realizing that writing a book is not as trivial as I imagined. This has some implications for my venture, since I regard the book as my first product. If I want to advocate the message of Entrepreneurial Mindfulness, I need to structure my ideas and make them accessible. Meanwhile, I will also have to finish my PhD. What could potentially go wrong? Well... I decided to practice what I preach. I will take my time for formal meditation, I will be mindful of my own needs, I will treat myself with compassion and I will create my version of the future from this present moment. If you are holding this book in your hands, you know that some parts of it worked out. With the experience of an MBSR training, I feel much more confident that I will able to enjoy this ride moment by moment, take each challenge at its time and cultivate my ability to remain a state of Being-while-Striving.

## My Mindful Awareness Attention Scale Score

Besides these weekly reflections, I also measured how mindful I was during the experiment and how this resembles my internal processes. Overall, I did not stop to *strive* to turn my ideas into reality, but I became more aware of my limits and became more content about the pace at which I can drive change. As mentioned in my diary, I experienced some significant changes in the way I approached my daily challenges and my aspirations of entrepreneurial striving. How does this translate in terms of my MAAS score?[30] Did I actually become "more mindful"? Well, let's just say it was a bumpy ride! Before I share it, let's have a look at the scale itself again.

As mentioned in Chapter 5, Kirk Warren Brown and Richard Ryan developed a set of 15 question to enable research on the effects of mindfulness on human functioning or the effect of mindfulness interventions on individuals' level of mindfulness. On a six-point scale ranging from "almost always" to "almost never", study participants rate the occurrence of mindfulness-related situations. "Almost never" would mean a numerical value of 6, whereas "almost always" would mean a 1. The higher the score, the more mindful you are. Feel free to have a look at the publicly available scale.

My mindfulness journey is best described in three phases. A phase of *overconfidence*, a little *mindfulness breakdown* and a phase of actually finding more *mental stillness*.

As you can see, I started with a solid 4.0. On average, I believed that I "somewhat infrequently" experienced unmindful moments. This went on for about two weeks. Interestingly, this score is quite close to the average result of 3.97, which Brown and Ryan measured in a random control group in their original study. Then, my experience got a bit more curious. By putting more and more attention on how mindfully I actually handled everyday situations, I figured out that I might not be as mindful as I thought. The realization of my initial "overconfidence" was followed by quite a bumpy mindfulness "breakdown". One day I felt that I was doing a good job of staying present, the next I felt like I failed horribly. My MBSR teacher suggested that mindfulness might also be a journey of uncomfortable truths. The realization that I am not as mindful as I thought was certainly one of them! "What did you do the Yoga teacher training for?" asked my ego. However, after another two to three weeks, I started to get my shit together. Things got more stable and I was increasingly able to recognize unmindful moments and return to being present.

# MY MBSR JOURNEY

*Figure 9: Illustration of my MAAS score during the MBSR course.*

Finally, I entered the "Zen" zone of my self-experiment. Settling down somewhere between 4.1 and 4.2, my average score got closer to the group of Zen practitioners in Brown and Ryan's study. The Zen practitioners averaged a score of 4.29. Especially with regard to questions 1, 3, 5, 8, 10 and 14, I was increasingly able to spot unmindful moments and returned to a mode of *being*. However, I still found it hard to stay mindful with regard to questions 2, 4 and 11. While the eight weeks of MBSR helped me to cultivate mindfulness in everyday life, I feel that these are my personal mindfulness nemeses. This is one of my biggest lessons from the program. Eight weeks will not fix habits or attentional patterns you have cultivated over decades. However, it is a highly effective starting point. A solid *mental reference point*.

Lastly, questions 9 and 13 neatly reflect the challenge of Being-while-Striving. These questions refer to staying mindful while pursuing goals and frequently dwelling on the past and the future. Like the questions from the last group, I believe that it takes a lot of dedicated practice to get mindfulness into these aspects of human functioning. By nature, entrepreneurs are goal-driven and focused on the future. They have to be. However, being conscious of it, being able to swiftly get back into a mode of *being* and enjoying the ride are surely desirable mental skills for changemakers. In summary, we see a bumpy ride, an overall trend towards becoming more mindful and some goals to work on.

Finally, how did my meditation practice and the respective internal development reflect in my well-being?

## My Well-Being

Every two weeks, I reflected on my subjective mental well-being by conducting the WHO-5 Well-Being Scale.[31] It is pretty straightforward and asks you to indicate your perceived situation for each of the five statements below. Evaluating the past two weeks, options for self-assessment include "all of the time", "most of the time", "more than half the time", "less than half the time", "some of the time" and "at no time".

1. ... I have felt cheerful and in good spirits

2. ... I have felt calm and relaxed

3. ... I have felt active and vigorous

4. ... I woke up feeling fresh and rested

5. ... My daily life has been filled with things that interest me

"All of the time" would have the numerical value of 5 and "at no time" would be a 0. Finally, the five values are added and multiplied by 4. Consequently, the best possible score equals 100 and the worst possible

# MY MBSR JOURNEY

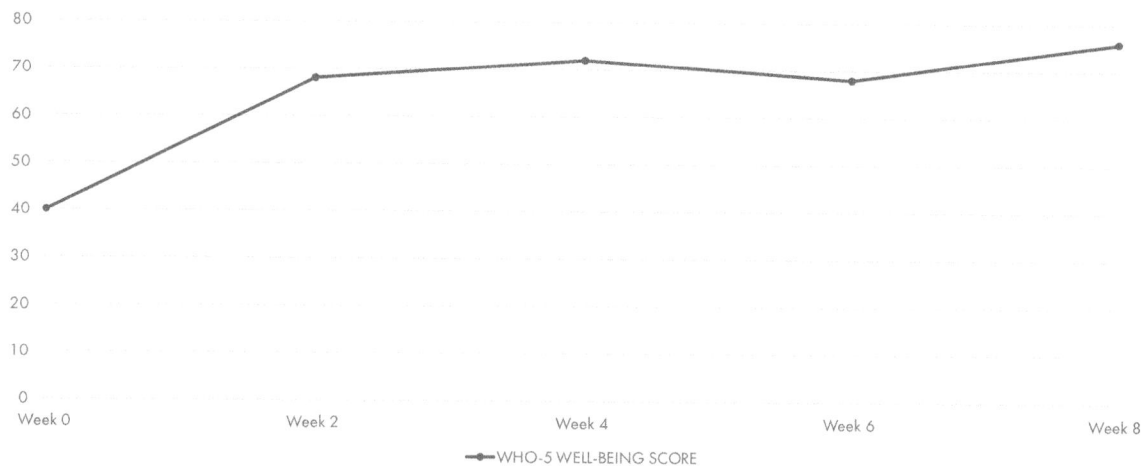

*Figure 10: Illustration of my WHO-5 Well-Being score during the MBSR course.*

score equals 0. My well-being developed much more smoothly and, generally speaking, I experienced highly positive effects during the MBSR program.

I started with a rather low score of 40, which was mainly due to bad sleep, a lot of worrying and being quite overwhelmed by all my tasks. However, it went up to a solid 72 in week four. I suggest that this was mainly due to better sleep and an improved ability to handle the stress of *striving*. I also focused more on positive events and developed my ability to stay mindful while striving for my goals. With a little bump around week six, I ended my MBSR self-experiment with a WHO-5 score of 76. Looking at the effect of mindfulness-based interventions from a review of the WHO-5 Well-Being Index, this seems to be at the extreme end of improvement.[32] However, I am usually a very content and energetic person and I started from a personal low. Anyway, in my MBSR self-experiment, I was able to experience and hence personally replicate the positive effects of a structured, systematic approach to meditation and mindfulness. Also, I provided some *anecdotal evidence* to support the idea of Being-while-Striving. I definitely believe that it is a worthwhile practice for every entrepreneur out there.

## In a Nutshell...

*Being-while-Striving...* I am still fascinated by this idea of creating the future while being conscious of doing so and remaining present. I think it is a wonderful concept and, even better, I have personally experienced it in real life. The reflection of my own MBSR experience in combination with previous academic work shows that Being-while-Striving might not be as incompatible as it intuitively seems. That being said, it is far from easy to implement it in everyday situations. It requires dedicated practice to develop the awareness of different cognitive modes and the self-regulation skills needed to deliberatively switch to the most appropriate one. Ideally, it would also be mentored by people who have already walked this road.

So, where do we stand on our journey of Entrepreneurial Mindfulness? From my own experience, I can now say that including formal meditation and mindfulness practice into the entrepreneurial journey can have huge benefits. I felt strongly positive effects on my well-being and *how* I did my work. However, I believe that *combining* mindfulness-based approaches and entrepreneurship-specific training might offer even more potential.

Interestingly, Lyddy and Good who pioneered the idea of Being-while-Doing, note that current mindfulness at work trainings usually apply practices that were developed in contemplative contexts, like meditation retreats.[33] Furthermore, they suggest that systematically integrating their findings about *being* and *doing* might help to develop more effective mindfulness practices for dynamic environments. For example, they propose that training should emphasize the skills of consciously recognizing and managing situations of *being*, *doing* or Being-while-Doing. Consequently, individuals might not just acquire mindfulness skills, but also learn to note when they are unmindful and become more able to deliberately return to mindfulness when desired.

But what about you? Can you become aware of your mental mode? Before proceeding to the last part of the book, let's run through another exercise. This one is inspired by the meditation technique of *mental noting*. If you get lost in *mind wandering* during meditation practice, you might want to apply the mental noting technique. For a short moment, intentionally focus your attention on the event that is distracting you, for example, "ah it's a thought", let it go and return to your meditation anchor, such as the breath, a body part or a visualization. However, mental noting is a technique that is performed in formal meditation practice. While formal meditation practice is essential, Entrepreneurial Mindfulness is still a matter of Being-while-Striving. It has to be transferred into the real life of changemakers. So, how might this be applied in everyday entrepreneurial settings?

# I Dare You:

## Name Your Mode!

- Have a look at the conceptual details of *being* and *striving* at the beginning of this chapter
- Take some time to reflect on how these modes are manifested in your personal experience
    - When do you get into a mode of *being*, and how does it feel for you?
    - When do you get into a mode of *striving*, and how does it feel for you?
    - When do you get into a mode of *Being-while-Striving*, how does it feel, and what triggers you to become entangled in pure *striving*?
- For the next week or so, try to be aware of these modes in your daily life
- Simply make a mental note
    - Ah, now I am in a mode of pure *being*
    - Ah, now I get carried away by my goals and ambitions
    - Ah, I am doing the things that I have to do, but calmly remaining aware of the present moment
- Occasionally, you might want to take a deep breath, let the intense moments of pure *striving* go and make space for an experience of *Being-while-Striving*
- This exercise is really about getting aware of the mode you are in and beginning the practice of consciously switching between them

# Entrepreneurial Mindfulness

We have come quite a long way together and learned a lot. This part of the book synthesizes the insights, concepts and experiences of the previous three parts. We have seen that our society relies on dedicated entrepreneurs to solve our global challenges. Our future truly depends on them. Yet, we also know that this responsibility might have severe effects on people's mental health and well-being. Recent scientific findings and the experiences I shared show that meditation and mindfulness practice might be an important tool for dealing with these challenges and might also make entrepreneurs more effective in pursuing their visions. Furthermore, mindfulness can also be thought of as *heartfulness*, which reveals *compassion* as an integral quality of Entrepreneurial Mindfulness. However, if changemakers are to create the future from the present moment with mindfulness, compassion and their whole self, they need to be empowered along their entire entrepreneurial journey. Therefore, in the next three chapters, I will develop ideas for how entrepreneurship training and education, entrepreneurial practice and innovation ecosystems can integrate the idea of Entrepreneurial Mindfulness.

## PART 04

"Vision is the art of seeing what is invisible to others."

JONATHAN SWIFT

# 07 The Entrepreneurial Mindfulness Training Program

A common denominator in several studies that I have discussed in the course of this book is the apparent potential of improved training and educational programs for entrepreneurs. This is not only intended to increase their effectiveness in helping entrepreneurs to start and grow businesses, but to enable a more *self-sustainable* way of driving change. Universities take a particularly important role in educating future entrepreneurs, and the scientific discussion about effective entrepreneurial education is in full swing. David Erler, one of my master's students, and I recently joined this discussion. For his thesis, David conducted and analyzed 36 interviews in the innovation ecosystems of Hamburg University of Technology and the University of Twente in the Netherlands. Based on his conversations with professors, students, founders and coaches, we wanted to understand how the University of Twente became one of the most entrepreneurial universities in Europe. Specifically, we analyzed the entrepreneurial journey from Chapter 3 and how measures such as entrepreneurship classes, events, accelerators and mentors support students in honing their entrepreneurial mindset. By the way, David is also a University Innovation Fellow! Since Entrepreneurial Mindfulness is supposed to empower entrepreneurs to create the future, honing the entrepreneurial mindset is an integral part of the idea. We need to understand how this "honing" works if we want to truly enrich it with the capacity for Being-while-Striving.

I will share some relevant scientific findings and then turn this chapter into an exercise of creative confidence. Based on the previous chapters, I will envision an Entrepreneurial Mindfulness Training Program: an approach to training future change-makers to drive sustainable change in a self-sustainable way. However, I will not leave it there. Because I don't trust my own *confirmation bias*, I will also challenge my ideas in a Deep Dive with Professor Yuval Engel, who is a pioneer in researching the effects of meditation on entrepreneurial behavior. Brace yourself; we have a lot to talk about!

## Honing the Entrepreneurial Mindset[1]

We are already familiar with the concept of an entrepreneurial journey and the mindsets that characterize certain cognitive orientations of entrepreneurs. Check Figure 4 in Chapter 3 for a little refresher. Different mindsets are activated when people take on the tasks associated with each phase of their entrepreneurial journey. The phases' tasks determine the characteristics of the relevant mindset.[2] Hence, in the early *predecisional* phase, the aspiring entrepreneur reflects his or her own wishes with regard to desirability and feasibility in order to decide on attractive, realistically attainable entrepreneurial opportunities.[3] As discussed, this implies a deliberative mindset. Nascent entrepreneurs need a broad range of information, which helps them to decide whether or not to pursue an entrepreneurial career or startup opportunity. In addition, support for a precise self-assessment of entrepreneurial skills and attitudes is required. This is where entrepreneurial education and training comes into play. Not surprisingly, research shows that offering educational programs, lectures, and courses specifically tailored to entrepreneurship supports formation of entrepreneurial intentions.[4] Nevertheless, the kinds of courses which are offered can make a significant difference. Experiential learning[5] seems to be particularly well suited. And design thinking[6] and business planning approaches[7] provide suitable frameworks in which to facilitate such training formats.

As we know, the entrepreneurial journey does not stop here. However, the effect of entrepreneurial education on forming entrepreneurial intentions seems to be much better understood than the effect on actually carrying them out. In the subsequent *preactional* and *actional* phases nascent entrepreneurs develop business plans and wait for suitable business opportunities to arise and take action in order to successfully create a venture. These tasks prime an implemental mindset, which supports cognitive processes when it comes to planning actual business execution.[8] Accordingly, the need of nascent entrepreneurs' for information and support becomes more utility-based and increasingly focuses on actually starting a business.[9] Here, nascent entrepreneurs need more hands-on guidance in the formulation of business plans, which help them to determine where to start, what to do and how to choose between options. Interestingly, training in self-control is beneficial when it comes to overcoming future difficulties on their entrepreneurial journey.[10] While the Entrepreneurial Mindfulness Training Program aims at nascent entrepreneurs, mindfulness should have a positive impact on entrepreneurial self-control, too (see Chapter 5). Entering the *post-actional* phase, the new entrepreneur resumes a process of deliberation.[11] Consequently, new entrepreneurs need support to evaluate the startup and its future directions, which is referred to as *elaborating growth intentions*.[12] In summary,

the entrepreneurial mindset involves adopting a deliberative, implemental and evaluative mindset according to the phase of the entrepreneurial journey. Different mindset characteristics determine the features of suitable educational and training support. Consequently, universities and other innovation ecosystems need to develop an integrated system of support offerings, which specifically target all aspects of the entrepreneurial mindset.[13]

This insight is important, because it implies that one approach, such as the Entrepreneurial Mindfulness Training Program, cannot support all stages of the entrepreneurial journey. Hence, this chapter and the Entrepreneurial Mindfulness Training Program are aimed at nascent entrepreneurs, for example in university or other educational contexts. However, it is surely not limited to the educational environment. The phenomenon of so-called "mumpreneurs" and many grassroots entrepreneurs show that you certainly don't need an entrepreneurship degree in order to become an entrepreneur. Other public institutions, NGOs or entrepreneurship related organizations, such as incubators or accelerators, are free to get inspired, too!

## The Synergy of Entrepreneurship and Mindfulness

Research and practice in the field of Entrepreneurial Mindfulness is yet to kick off fully. Therefore, I formulated my four propositions and am hoping to inspire further exploration. I believe that integrating mindfulness and meditation into entrepreneurship training and education can have a positive impact on three crucial challenges. One that concerns all of us, one that concerns the venture's success and one that concerns the entrepreneur.

Let's briefly recall the propositions. The first of my propositions has to do with the challenges that mindful entrepreneurs decide to tackle. I believe that cultivating mindfulness through meditation will lead entrepreneurs to pursue more socially- or sustainability-driven purposes. This means they are more likely to tackle the societal challenges that we all face. Yuval Engel was the first researcher to show empirical evidence for this relationship[14] and we will discuss it in more detail later. Secondly, I believe that cultivating mindfulness through meditation results in more consistent action on the goals which result from someone's purpose. Marco von Gelderen and colleagues showed that more mindful individuals are generally less likely to engage in entrepreneurial action.[15] However, when they do and they have previous experience, they take even more action than less mindful individuals. So, they do think twice but, if they decide to go for it, they build on their experiences and act more consistently with their goals. In line with scientific findings on honing the entrepreneurial mindset, I think that an Entrepreneurial Mindfulness Training Program should also entail practical entrepreneurship training. This way, the cultivation of mindfulness is directly coupled with some degree of entrepreneurial experience. At the end of the day, entrepreneurs have to get a viable business running... This leads us to my third proposition on the quality of entrepreneurial decision-making. By gaining more clarity about present internal and external events, mindful entrepreneurs should also become better decision-makers.

Lastly, I believe that cultivating mindfulness through meditation has a positive effect on maintaining well-being while pursuing goals related to entrepreneurial ventures. This relates to the internal challenge of entrepreneurs and social entrepreneurs in particular. They have to get a business running while striving to make a positive societal impact. The positive impact of meditation and mindfulness practice on dealing with stress, anxiety and promoting various mental health aspects has been confirmed in numerous empirical studies.[16] Again, Yuval Engel and his colleagues showed the first evidence on this mechanism in the context of entrepreneurial *fear of failure*.[17] Indeed, in 2019, MIT Sloan launched one of the first programs to combine entrepreneurship education with a particular focus on participants' *self-awareness*. The program also included meditation and mindfulness elements. Surveying 60 participants before and after the program, MIT Sloan found that at the end of the program:[18]

- 93% indicated that practicing self-awareness can help entrepreneurs create more successful ventures
- 88% had established their personal systematic mindfulness or meditation practice
- 53% were more frequently using specific tools to cope with stress
- 40% were more aware of their emotional experience than before

## Envisioning an Entrepreneurial Mindfulness Training Program

Based on the three challenges which I outlined earlier, the four propositions, my own MBSR self-experiment and over ten years of studying innovation and entrepreneurship, I want to conduct an exercise of creative confidence and propose an Entrepreneurial Mindfulness Training Program — a journey of learning to create the future from the present moment, and of Being-while-Striving. I imagine an engaging experience that inspires nascent change-makers to tackle important societal challenges. The program will equip them with an adequate skill set as well as mindset to tackle their internal and external challenges. We don't know all the details about how and why the MBSR program works. However, we know that it works, and I am a big fan of *stealing with pride*. Why reinvent the wheel? Hence, I am thinking about an eight-week program and an initial full day of inspiration. After all, the intensity and duration of MBSR seems to do a decent job!

However, we are obviously talking about Entrepreneurial Mindfulness and not solely about mindfulness. Consequently, certain topics in the context of mindfulness need to be complemented with other tools and attitudes. Based on my research and interviews, I am thinking about the following content, skills and mindsets:

- Inspiration for our societal challenge
  - Input about the United Nation's 17 Sustainable Development Goals (SDGs) to prime a sustainability-driven purpose
- Meditation for the internal challenge
  - Bodyscan to cultivate self-awareness
  - Loving-kindness meditation to cultivate compassion for the self and the global environment
  - Mindful movement for physical as well as emotional awareness and well-being
  - Breathing meditation to cultivate control of attention and self-regulation
- Toolset to tackle the external challenge
  - Business *model canvas* to break down the complexity of a startup
  - Design *thinking* to develop convincing value propositions, cultivate creative confidence and put empathy into action
  - Customer *journey mapping* to understand users' or beneficiaries' experience of engaging with a business
- Inner qualities of Entrepreneurial Mindfulness
  - An entrepreneurial mindset
  - A strong sense of purpose
  - A growth mindset
  - Awareness of and ability to maintain a state of Being-while-Striving
  - Empathy, compassion and self-compassion
  - Emotional literacy and self-regulation
  - Self-responsibility

Let me guide you through my vision how aspiring changemakers could get there.

## Eight-Week Entrepreneurial Mindfulness Training Program

### Week 1 - The Core of Being-While-Striving

The first week features a kick-off in form of an inspiring full day event. This includes an introduction to the topic of entrepreneurship and why it is crucial for tackling societal challenges, such as the 17 SDGs. Watching David Attenborough's new movie *A Life On Our Planet* would wonderfully set the stage for the topic of how to envision a better future and telling a compelling story about it. Indeed, I did a sneaky little experiment with my students. In my *empathic communication* class, we watched the movie and the students' assignment was to pick one SDG, develop their own change vision about it and tell a compelling story in a TED style event. It was great fun and the students totally connected to the goals.

As well as being a little nudge into sustainability-driven entrepreneurship, this kick-off introduces the topic of well-being, mindfulness in the context of workplace settings and the idea of Being-while-Striving. A Yoga and meditation session will practically introduce all four of the core meditation techniques and show how mindfulness and compassion can be cultivated. Finally, the Entrepreneurial Mindfulness Diagram will be introduced. Time for reflection on passions, strengths and values in small groups would finally kick off the journey. Further individual reflection on the Entrepreneurial Mindfulness Diagram and research on the SDGs would mark the informal practice until week 2. Lastly, a 20-minute commitment to guided body scans would be the formal meditation for Week 1 and 2.

## Week 2 – The Purpose-Driven Business Model Canvas

This week builds on selecting one of the 17 SDGs for an entrepreneurial project for the remainder of the program. Based on research and reflection, participants select a goal and form a founding team around this strategic priority. What is their entrepreneurial purpose? The *purpose-driven business model canvas* from Chapter 3 would provide the first hands-on tool for handling the complexity of new ventures and getting an idea about entrepreneurial tasks. The team would take on the challenge of constantly updating the canvas during the program. Because the multitude of challenges might be quite intimidating, this is the right time for a growth mindset intervention. Growth mindset interventions have been shown to increase perceived entrepreneurial self-efficacy in a study by Jeni Burnette and colleagues.[19] Let's hone the entrepreneurial mindset! The task until week 3 would be to research opportunities for impact and select a specific challenge to develop a *value hypothesis.*: a central assumption about an offering, which solves a customer's or beneficiary's problem.

## Week 3 – Design Thinking and Empathy

Developing a *value hypothesis* into a *value proposition*, which can be a product, service or experience is a highly creative process. However, it should be closely aligned to the users' needs and context. The most elaborated methodology I know for facilitating this process of creating empathy, developing wild ideas and testing them is design thinking.[20] We will get into more detail about design thinking in Chapter 9. As discussed, research also suggests it to be well suited to honing the entrepreneurial mindset.[21] The University Innovation Fellows program, which I mentioned several times, strongly builds on this methodology. It is hosted by one of the global design thinking hubs, the Hasso Plattner Institute of Design at Stanford University. Guiding students through the process as a mentor in the program allowed me to see the effects of well-executed educational design thinking experiences first hand. An introduction of the design thinking process and the consequent task of applying it to an opportunity for impact is at the core of this session. Since the design thinking process covers several steps, it will guide the entrepreneurial action part of things for the next two weeks. Loving-kindness meditation is a great tool for creating empathy[22] and will mark this week's meditation impulse. A daily loving-kindness meditation practice will guide the next two weeks of formal meditation.

## Week 4 – Digging Deeper

Let's see what ideating and testing the value hypotheses resulted in! Based on that, we should get a clearer understanding about the other components of the purpose-driven business model canvas. What would be necessary key activities, resources and partnerships? What drives revenues and cost structure? There would be an interactive session for teamwork, open questions, reflection and feedback for the ongoing design thinking process.

## Week 5 – Self-Awareness and Well-Being

Well, that is quite a lot of input and *striving*. Let's practice what we preach and mind our own capacity. This week will deal with the concept of well-being in more detail. What matters to changemakers' mental, physical and social well-being? Are participants always able to maintain all of these facets? What can we learn from mindfulness at work? A deep dive into goal intentions and habits will provide participants with tools to build up long-lasting strategies to cope with a challenging entrepreneurial marathon. The formal practice will entail a series of Yoga-based mindful movements.

## Week 6 – Emotional Literacy and User Experiences

Now participants have developed an understanding of the complexity of new ventures and how a value proposition for their target group, how can they deliver this value? Sure, startups will ultimately have to solve many crucial challenges. However, I think that this is a suitable last challenge for an eight-week entrepreneurship sprint. I am a big fan of mapping customer journeys to facilitate the design of engaging *user experiences*. Getting an idea of the goals, thoughts and emotions that drive your customers' or beneficiaries' behavior is crucial.

I personally applied this approach in a critical environment. At Hamburg University of Technology, I took the role of a *user experience manager* for a master's degree in innovation management and entrepreneurship. Students from all around the globe trusted us with their future and mostly interacted with us online for the first part of their journey. Understanding their hopes, fears and aspirations was critical to gaining their trust and supporting them with all the information they needed to make the best decision for their future. This decision could of course mean that our program was not the perfect fit for them. I believe that we had an amazing product, but creating awareness and guiding our customers towards a decision was equally crucial. An introduction to customer journey mapping will be accompanied by the concept of emotional literacy. How can you design for a customer's experience if you can't articulate the emotions you are trying to cater for? Formal practice will complement the movement practice with the naming technique from Chapter 6. What is coming up in the practice? Is it a thought? An emotion? What kind of emotion? Frustration? Joy? This will introduce the idea that introspection is a tool to cultivate awareness of emotions and emotional literacy!

## Week 7 – Finding Stillness in a World in Motion

Let's see what the customer journey mapping method uncovered. What could be suitable ways to integrate the value proposition into engaging user experiences? A last interactive session to finalize the purpose-driven business model canvas and prepare a change vision for week 8. As a last formal meditation tool, breathing meditation will be introduced. Simple, but challenging, it is an amazing tool for cultivating attention-related aspects of mindfulness practice. Because it is so challenging to come to terms with the "monkey mind" and take the observer's seat, I chose this as the last formal meditation technique. But mastering pure non-doing bears amazing potential for entrepreneurs. With enough practice, we can learn to better deal with whatever challenge life throws at us by sitting down, accepting what comes up, focusing on our breath and returning to calmness. Are participants up for a challenge for 20 minutes of daily breathing meditation during a potentially intense last week and beyond?

## Week 8 – Celebrating the Future and Savoring the Present Moment

Time to celebrate innovation and share engaging change visions in a pitching session! A first-hand experience of how creativity and collaboration are channeled into visions and solutions for a better future. Sure, an eight-week program can only be considered an entrepreneurial sprint where, as we have seen, entrepreneurship is ultimately a marathon. How might this marathon look like and how could the mindfulness and meditation components of our training help with that? There will be a last reflection on the program and a challenge to take the ideas and practice forward into a journey of creating the future from the present moment, and of Being-while-Striving.

Looking at the initial list of tools, inner qualities and methods, this program would pretty much cover everything that I have discussed in this book so far. It is also based on research in many aspects, and it is still a product of my imagination. Let's walk the talk, get some first feedback on the program and see what other support entrepreneurs might need in later phases of their journey. We will do that in a conversation with a true expert and pioneer in the field of combining the worlds of entrepreneurship and meditation, Professor Yuval Engel.

# Deep Dive

## A Conversation with Yuval Engel,
## the Pioneering Meditation Researcher

Malte: Yuval, thank you so much for taking your time to have this conversation with me! Let's dive right into it! My first question is — how did you end up becoming a professor for entrepreneurship and then how did the topic of meditation come into play?

Yuval: OK... It's a very strange and long story! I will to try to keep it short. I will start with the meditation part, because it kind of overlaps in the timeline. My interest in it started paradoxically enough when I was in the military. I spend some years in the Israeli army. I was a sniper and did a lot of breath work as part of my training, but I was not really aware of where it came from. The focus was simply on how to shoot better when you have less air in you or breathing very fast and so on. But it weirdly caught some of my interest. Later on, I was in my bachelor's and already here in Amsterdam, I had this course, which was by far the best course that I ever took in university.

Malte: Now I'm curious!

Yuval: I was in a newly founded honors program and they offered courses by the best professors of the university to a very small group of students. I had a lot of privilege to visit these courses. Usually, I studied business, which is kind of boring, and then suddenly I had a course with a neuroscientist, a philosopher and a theologian. It was a course about consciousness in Western and Eastern schools of thought. It was really spot on and covered a lot of everything from Hindu and Buddhist texts, and from Sanskrit to modern philosophy of neuroscience. It was about understanding consciousness and where it is located in the brain, if at all. That piqued my intellectual interest.

At that point I was not doing any meditation! I just started being exposed to the idea. And then as part of this course, we also went to a Zen center for a session. It was a field visit and we did a one-hour meditation. Out of the blue, you know. Now, I am thinking that it was strange, because Zen is kind of strict. It was a very rigid atmosphere. You're just supposed to sit in a certain way, there was no movement, very little guidance and a lot of these visual statues as targets. Very organized... Which I think is the most unfriendly way to start a meditation practice, probably. But it was my first experience in trying it out. From that point of first trying it, it took me maybe three or four more years of reading around it. Instead of actually doing it... And I had a classic entry in that I was trying it out while having a life crisis. I had a very bad break-up from a long-term relationship.

Malte: Well, I've been there, too! It forces you to find better ways of handling the unpleasant emotions and thoughts.

Yuval: Yeah, and since then, that was probably ten years ago, I was having some kind of a meditation practice. With varying magnitudes of emphasis, of course. I think that I had a good two-year break when my son was born. In this early time, I could just not find any way or time. There was a time when I used to do it in my sleep. Sort of when you wake up at night, and you automatically go in this mode. But even that disappeared for a while. Now, I am more or less stabilized in a rhythm. I mostly do morning mediation after

I take my son to kindergarten. I have a nice stop in the park.

Malte: That sounds like a really nice meditation spot.

Yuval: Yes, it is! And that's the meditation part. I didn't say anything about entrepreneurship yet. I also got into it as less of a planned thing. But maybe those lines will connect somehow. I actually didn't plan to study in the Netherlands. I met a girl that I was travelling with somewhere in New Zealand and Australia. I was away for a year.

Malte: So, the classic post-army travel trip?

Yuval: Yeah! I went very, very far from Israel. That was the main idea. And then I went back home after 10 months or so. I was in this "in between stage". I was just coming back, but it was clear that I was at an age at which I should make some choices about my life. And I was very unhappy with the idea of making choices about my life! So, I thought, well... there was this girl I met back in New Zealand. She lives in Amsterdam and I have never been to Amsterdam. I had no work permit or anything and I didn't even think about this stuff. I just thought, well, hang around, work in a bar, see what happens... The concept of having a CV didn't really strike me. It was wonderful naivety. Anyway, after a couple of months, I realized that my status here was becoming very illegal, very soon. I had to do something about it and I found that the only legal solution to stick around here was to become a student. I got into business studies and from there I glided a bit with the system. I finished my bachelor's and then again, out of not wanting to choose I continued. I thought, well, it's a one-year master so I can just continue and move along. At the end of this master's, I had my thesis, which was about entrepreneurship. So, by then I had some kind of interest in the topic. I am not entirely sure why... I think because it was newer, more exciting than other topics that I was studying. I felt some connection there and retrospectively, I would say that I am interested in uncertainty and how people deal with it. I think this shifted me over to this discipline because it has a lot of it! I also think that's where entrepreneurship and meditation connects. Then, I did my PhD at the VU University in Amsterdam, where I had also studied earlier. I moved to the University of Amsterdam as an assistant professor and I got into this hyper-competitive system. One of the things I did was to take the interest in meditation and bringing it over to entrepreneurship. That was one of the topics that I was more personally connected to.

It is obvious when you're in it. If you know both of these worlds, it's almost like you don't need to speak about it. It's a natural connection. But for people who don't know either... When you are in entrepreneurship and I tell you about a project about meditation, it sounds very "out there". It's not really business-related. And if you are doing mediation and you are trying to connect it to the commercialization aspect of entrepreneurship, it sounds almost "dirty". From a spiritual perspective. I think what I was trying to do was to bring these two things together in a way that makes sense to people. That's why I think the topics of my studies were as they were. The combination of self-compassion and fear of failure, for example. For me, that was just the easiest entry point. Fear of failure in that sense was the easiest connection. Because this connects with well-being, and there is quite a lot of evidence about meditation as a technique for stress reduction, for example. So it kind of overlaps in a way that people can easily understand. Apart from the fact that I think that self-compassion is an underutilized concept, overall. Like, I am really... It's a strange word to use, but "I dig it"! It's one of these things that you intuitively understand.

Malte: I believe that everybody does! As you said, this Zen mediation may not be a good entrance, but I feel like if you do a good loving-kindness meditation with people, they get it. When you use everyday words, like – "So many times, we are really hard on ourselves. Take some minutes to let that go and from there, take this to other people!" I started doing that in my lecture and some workshops this year, too. Just to practice what I preach and yeah... people get it. There was nobody who said, what are we doing here?

Yuval: I have been teaching it now for three years or so. In my startup psychology course, I always do a series of meditations. I give them recorded meditations and I let them practice. I let them do a body scan, a breath meditation and a loving-kindness meditation. Sort of to give a tasting menu. Still, I do get very extreme responses to it. Most of the students are somewhere in between. There are the ones who super love it and are very connected to it. Then, there are the ones who really could not stand it. They do not understand why I am doing this. It is boring for them. But some get the point of connecting entrepreneurship and meditation. I don't want to sound too dogmatic about it. Other people might think differently about it. I do think it's an almost obvious connection when you do put things together in a way. What entrepreneurs do, what kind of problems they deal with. It's almost like an extreme version of what humans do. Right? We all have experiences that are similar to what entrepreneurs do in work or in life or in other elements. But starting a company by yourself or with a small group of people and trying to sell something new to the world... It just pushes it to a level where people are bound to deal with things that require some peacefulness.

Malte: I think that this is a great way to put it. Entrepreneurship is an extreme form of being human. I also believe that entrepreneurs can benefit a lot from meditation. Let's dig a bit deeper into this connection. I have some ideas I wanted to share with you and that go in the direction of what you already said. I condensed three entrepreneurial challenges on which meditation and mindfulness could have a positive impact. You actually already researched two of them. One challenge that I see is the societal challenge. You know, everything related to the 17 Sustainable Development Goals. I feel like it's a good point at which to start looking for entrepreneurial opportunities. We need entrepreneurs to deal with that, at the end of the day, right? We need people who come up with solutions and you already showed that, for example, loving-kindness meditations can result in more sustainability-driven decision-making. That's the one part. The second part would be that, when you get into meditation and start the cultivation of focusing your attention and practice self-regulation, you are more likely to follow up on the goals that you set. That would be for me the second challenge. Actually maintaining the volition of getting a viable business running. The third one would be the internal challenge. Related to the study you did on how self-compassion helps with anxiety. I see these three entrepreneurial challenges. The societal one, the external challenge and the internal one. I believe that mindfulness and meditation can potentially have a positive impact on that. How do you feel about this framing? Is there anything you would add to that?

Yuval: You know, I am adding my own biases here. These days, my main focus is studying diversity and mainly gender equality in startup employee recruitment. I am also sort of seeing an entry point there. There are some studies that show that meditation might help. Because when you create this sort of little space in between some trigger and a response, right... You have more control of that. That also speaks to things like stereotypes, and quick judgments about other people. There are studies that show that meditation practice can also influence the way that we categorize things or reduce biases, stereotyping and so on. So, I also think that this is another touchpoint around that issue. Talking about, for example, gender bias in entrepreneurship and so on, most of the studies are busy with this interface between investors and entrepreneurs. There is a ton of studies about investor gender bias. Or women who think that they are not fitting in some kind of a mold that would apply for high-growth entrepreneurship, for example. And I think that another element of it is that entrepreneurs actually do the same to the people they choose to work with, like employees or co-founders.

Because there is another selection interface. If you are a startup founder and you start growing, you are bound to deal with hiring decisions. Hence, you are selecting people to bring into the organization. Most entrepreneurs are both young-ish and inexperienced in doing this and they take a long time to realize that they need to hire a professional to work on that element of their company. Other things entrepreneurs do, it's based a lot on intuition or acting quickly and I feel meditation might also enter the picture here. It is again a bit of a paradox. It puts a pause into a lot of decisions that entrepreneurs tend to do very quickly. Without over-analyzing it. I don't have any empirical examples for it, yet. But I suspect that theoretically, it is a direction that is possible to look at. For example, how do entrepreneurs make certain decisions around hiring or it could also be in team elements. If they practice meditation, these decisions might be different than if they are not. But that's just my own sort of interest mingled together. Can you repeat your second point? Because you had the point about internal processes, you had the point about society and then the second one was?

Malte: Yeah, the external challenge of actually getting the business running and sticking to your goals. I am quite involved with goal intentions and the theory of planned behavior because I am applying it in my PhD thesis. So it is about following up on set goal intentions, which is basically getting through the challenges of getting the business running.

Yuval: Yeah, it's funny. There is this study, I always find it very funny that it is this combination of self-regulation, goal pursuit and meditation. But it is combined in a way that I didn't think of before. The title is, "Mindfulness, Meet Self-Regulation", and they use self-regulation techniques in order to sustain a meditation practice.[23] So, it is upside-down from the way I would have imagined. I would have imagined meditation to influence goal pursuit intentions. But they flipped it around and they say, here is what we know from Western science about how to keep your goals and making sure that you are actually following up on them. We apply it to meditation practice in order to make sure people sustain a meditation practice.

Malte: OK, so formulating a goal intention for an upcoming time period, like "I will meditate so and so long..."

Yuval: Yeah, something like that. This topic of self-regulation also involves the sense of setting intentions and actually following up on your goals — it is a lot of what I do with my students. So, the whole action planning and implementation intentions. I think that is a good point of connection, too. There are a lot of things in entrepreneurship around decision-making that are easily related to meditation from this self-awareness, self-regulation type. I did my PhD on effectuation. There is this string of decision-making writing that is akin to The *Lean Startup*. It is focusing on experimentation, action first, planning later and emergent plans. Effectuation is sort of means oriented. You start with what you have rather than with a goal, you know? I find meditation relates to that in a couple of ways. One is in this idea of meta-cognition. So, knowing when to apply what decision-making technique, to which situation. Sometimes, you do need a lot of planning, and other times you really need to go for it and the trick is to know when. I think that meditation has a lot of elements that speak to that decision of being aware of – "In which situation am I in? Who am I? What can I do in this situation?" Because applying the same technique to all situations always ends up badly... But again, these are all assumptions.

Malte: So you have more assumptions and you are planning to explore the connection of entrepreneurship and meditation even more?

Yuval: Yeah, I mean the planning is the difficult part. I always keep it as a focus next to all the stuff I do. So, when I have an opportunity for a study that I cannot ignore, that sticks in my brain, I will do it! For now, I have only one ongoing project that has a meditation element to it. I am a little bit tired of doing these small hypothetical experiments of very short meditation interventions and I want to expand it. Something more complex with a full-on meditation program over time. It's just that this kind of program is challenging from a practical perspective.

Malte: Maybe, I come into play here... To give you a little bit more of a background, I am involved in a program, which is called the University Innovation Fellows. It is a program by the d.school in Stanford and they do it every year. The program is focused on students, driving change at their campuses. They are running through a six-week program, where they get to know tools like the business model canvas, design thinking and so on. They are learning these tools and then they are challenged to pick up a project and actually drive change at their university. At Hamburg University of Technology, we are doing this in our third year now and I am one of the faculty mentors. I am guiding the students from our side and it is very inspiring how the d.school team runs the program. Complementary to that, I recently did a MBSR training myself and I saw how well this structured approach to meditation works. I thought it would be cool to combine these two approaches and come up with an Entrepreneurial Mindfulness Training Program. It might create a more solid basis for testing the interplay of both worlds. It would be a cool environment in which to challenge hypotheses about how mindfulness and entrepreneurship could be connected. In this case, it would be more in the field of education, as I am quite engaged with universities. I actually drafted a program for how this could look like. On the one hand, it would involve teaching tools like the business model canvas, design thinking and customer journey mapping to have a foundation for how to tackle important entrepreneurial challenges. But also, at the same time, it would involve the essential meditation techniques you mentioned, like breathing meditations, body scans, and loving-kindness. I am a Yoga teacher, so I can teach Yoga. That's my idea at the moment. How do you feel about that?

Yuval: Yeah, I think it is great. So, what is the goal of the program? And then the crowd for this program would be university people?

Malte: I think, it would be students, yes. But I also talked to a friend of mine, who went through several accelerator programs; he said that all this meditation and everything related to self-awareness was never a topic. At least, when he did it. He learned the hard way to take care of himself. He said that meditation helped him. Therefore, I think that accelerators and incubators could also benefit from having something more structured.

Yuval: Yeah, I really think that's a nice direction. But then I wonder if... Well, I am not entirely sure about the combination of working with lean methodology, the business model canvas and customer journeys and doing the meditations for entrepreneurs in action. I would think that, especially for accelerators or incubators, the selling point would be more in line with this — you want to prepare these people for the challenges of being in an acceleration program, right? You know, this "condenser". The accelerators prepare them with coaching on practical elements, like coding sometimes or doing some classes about canvases and so on. But these meditation and Yoga type things are a slightly different type of help, right? It is to help them deal with their internal processes. And I think that step where you combine it with canvases and other business-related elements is maybe a second step. Where it sort of awaits testing. Because I don't know what would be a hypothesis about combining the business model canvas with meditation... Assuming that you have a perfect experimental design where you have two identical batches in an accelerator, one is doing your program and the other one is just doing the business model canvas program without the meditation. What would you expect the difference to be?

Malte: I think you have a really good point. They are different target groups. So, people who are already in the incubator are already entrepreneurs, and then, there is my idea about students who are probably interested in entrepreneurship in general and that this program would spark their entrepreneurial mindset. So, I think there are two different discussions. From what I imagined, when you take this into the university environment, the outcome would be that sustainability-driven entrepreneurial intentions would grow among students. In addition, there is the idea of entrepreneurial well-being with regard to meditation. If they follow up on these newly formed entrepreneurial intentions, they already have the tools to take responsibility for their own well-being. That is my idea on that side. And I think you are very right that for accelerators the program would probably look different.

Yuval: Yeah, I would call it something like a mental resilience program for accelerators. So, like getting away from the marketing as a spiritual practice and doing it more like psychological support on your entrepreneurial journey. Then I think the interesting part would be how to... So, if you just do regular meditation techniques or some standard meditations or Yoga practice, you don't really have an edge over any other meditation training! But since you are actually bringing these two worlds together, and you have knowledge of how both worlds work, I think it's nicer to have some kind of... Something specifically structured that makes it more applicable for entrepreneurs. I don't know what this thing might be. I am just brainstorming right now.

Malte: Well, I might have an idea of what that thing could be, too. There is this paper from Marco van Gelderen. Basically, it's the third empirical study on entrepreneurship and mindfulness after your two studies. In the context of Entrepreneurial Mindfulness, I am talking about creating the future from the present moment and I see a bit of a paradox there. Because mindfulness is very much about being in the present moment, whereas in entrepreneurship and innovation, you have to think about the future. You have to plan to some extent or at least envision the future. Even if you are more in this effectuation mode, you somehow have to deal with that. Marco van Gelderen and colleagues address this paradox with the term *Being-while-Striving*, which I really like. If there could be something about that, like a very specific meditation technique. I am not aware of anything, but it could be a cool thing!

Yuval: Yeah, I will definitely think about it, because it also relates to everything I do and I work with Marco. We sometimes talk about this stuff. I can also ask him what he thinks about it; he is teaching a course about entrepreneurial skills. It's sort of about "being" an entrepreneur. It combines all of it nicely together. This could be really nice. Just from what I heard you say, I personally find the idea of a program tailored for accelerators a lot more tempting than the university-based option of getting students into entrepreneurship. Apart from one thing. The people I work with in the project, which I told you about in my current meditation study, they are coming from these entrepreneurial education topics. They are really interested in how meditation can possibly change the entrepreneurial identity of students. Pushing them more from a "Darwinist" type of business-oriented focus to a more social or sustainable focus. That sort of rings a bell. But maybe it's just me.... I find the accelerator thing more appealing. I see that some accelerators have these external freelancers that are doing some Yoga or meditation, but it's not really a core part of the program and I feel there is room for it. So, if you come up with something that is slightly more unique than the next freelancer or Yoga teacher, it will be really cool. If you move along with an idea and you have some things you want to talk about, I am happy to brainstorm and I will think about it. I am also interested in this direction.

Malte: Yeah, for sure! Well, the University Innovation Fellow project will be one part of my journey anyway. Everything around university students and sparking their entrepreneurial mindset. But I agree with you that there are entrepreneurs out there who are facing this internal challenge, and they already know more about the "entrepreneurial doing" part. For me, one key outcome is that there must be two distinct approaches. But I like you, and I like the idea. I am definitely up for it!

## In a Nutshell...

Well, that was a true Deep Dive! As you can see, reality is often more complex than expected. As with the complexity of an entrepreneurial journey, one approach to Entrepreneurial Mindfulness will not solve all the challenges that changemakers face. While some aspects of making Entrepreneurial Mindfulness a thing must await further investigation, I feel like we learned some important lessons. Firstly, the combination of entrepreneurship and mindfulness still offers room for exploration and potential synergies. For example, the effect of meditation on entrepreneurial decision-making and related biases is an exciting area. Secondly, specific interventions are needed to understand and test these relationships. Currently, research tends to build on traditional meditation training but does not adapt them to the specific entrepreneurial context. Thirdly, along their journey, entrepreneurs deal with different challenges, so the combination of entrepreneurship and mindfulness might take different shapes depending on the phase of the journey. Respective entrepreneurial education and training should take the specific context into consideration and provide different approaches depending on that very context. This chapter was an exercise of creative confidence, as I obviously don't know the results and effects of combining the education of nascent entrepreneurs with meditation practices in an Entrepreneurial Mindfulness Training Program. However, from everything I learned in this journey, I am surely willing to try! If anyone out there is with me, feel free to reach out!

An eight-week course is feasible in the context of a university class or similar. Entrepreneurs that are already engaged in getting a business running might be less patient and have very real everyday challenges to solve. Here, an intervention might need to be more condensed and utility-based. While Yuval's personal interest gravitates towards the support of entrepreneurs in the field, I am happy that he acknowledges the potential of enriching entrepreneurial training with mindfulness and meditation. Nevertheless, I said that I would challenge my ideas and I am happy to take Yuval's feedback into the remainder of this book. The Entrepreneurial Mindfulness Training Program can apparently just cover a part of the entrepreneurial journey. So, in the next chapter, we will dive deeper into the mechanics of mindfulness and its role in mitigating the effects of stressful work environments. Based on that, we will learn how entrepreneurs might benefit from dedicated support programs that build on meditation and mindfulness. You may have guessed that the last exercises of this book progressively point in that direction. Let's do another one!

# I Dare You:

Journal Your Emotions!

- In the last exercise, I asked you to get aware of the mode you are in, and we will build on that
- Prepare a little journaling exercise for the upcoming week
  - Keep your journal, in whatever medium you choose, in graspable distance for real time data collection
- This time, turn your attention to the emotions that arise when you are in specific situations and specifically name these emotions
  - Journal about phases in which you are motivated, engaged and focused
  - Journal about phases in which you take time to recover, nurture and connect with yourself and others
  - Journal about phases in which you are hard on yourself, worry about the future or are anxious and stressed out
- Additionally, try to keep track of the activities or situations that trigger your systems
  - Cookie points: Is there a space in which you can control how your emotional response affects your behavioral response?
- Reflect on your journal and find imbalances
- What can you do to create more balance in your daily life?
  - Can you avoid unnecessary stress or deal with it in a more self-compassionate way?
  - Can you control your inner response to challenging situations?
  - Can you make time for nurturing activities?

"The best way
to find yourself
is to lose yourself
in the service
of others."

MOHANDAS KARAMCHAND GANDHI

# 08 The Mindful Startup

As we know now, entrepreneurs may need very different support than aspiring changemakers in educational contexts. In that sense, entrepreneurs need to learn how not to entirely lose themselves in the service of others or in the service of their venture. Building on the initial thoughts from the introduction of this book and what we have learned so far, I propose that a *mindful startup* mindfully navigates its founders' inherent exposure to conditions of extreme uncertainty, thus allowing them to take their whole selves on a fulfilling entrepreneurial journey.

By now, we know much more about the inherent conditions of extreme uncertainty and their potentially harmful effects on entrepreneurial well-being. We also know that meditation and mindfulness practice can be important resources in that context. However, we did not discuss how the founders of startups could implement a dedicated approach to mindfulness in their working life. The previous discussions about mindfulness were of more general nature. Now, we will build on our better understanding of the world of entrepreneurs and go into more detail about *mindfulness at work*.

Obviously, mindfulness is not new to the world of busy people. However, it has received much more attention in other contexts than in the context of entrepreneurship and startups. Managers, leaders and busy employees suffer from stressful work environments or constant information overload too. Mindfulness interventions in workplace settings have skyrocketed in recent years and academic research has confirmed its effectiveness in numerous ways.[24] Plenty of positive effects have been confirmed and this might inform entrepreneurship-focused programs. We will discuss several insights from research into mindfulness in the workplace, and then enrich mindfulness with the idea of *compassion*. Finally, we will have a Deep Dive with a true mindfulness expert and entrepreneur, Hanna Tempelhagen. Hanna is a co-founder of The Mindful Spaces in Hamburg, the certified MBSR teacher who guided my MBSR self-experiment and, most importantly, a human being with a unique story about how she got to this point.

## Entrepreneurs' Unique Challenges

Before we look into mindfulness in the context of stressful work environments, we need to examine the unique context of startups and entrepreneurs. In one of the few studies on entrepreneurship and mindfulness, which was published in 2019, Marco van Gelderen and colleagues suggest that mindfulness is largely underexplored in the context of entrepreneurship.[25] However, they stress the fact that mindfulness has generally been shown to be beneficial in other business settings. They refer to the review by Darren Good and colleagues, which summarizes positive effects of mindfulness in the workplace and provides a comprehensive analysis of the underlying mechanisms.[26] We will have a closer look at these mechanisms in the next section. Building on the scientific foundations of entrepreneurship research, Marco van Gelderen and his co-authors suggest that entrepreneurship is particularly characterized by a *very dynamic* work environment. More specifically, starting a new business venture involves *risk* and *uncertainty*, it requires founders to succeed in an array of challenging tasks and it is accompanied by various interpersonal and contextual factors. On the one hand, this is comparable to other challenging job environments. So to some degree, we can assume that mindfulness is indeed relevant to the entrepreneurial context and that previous findings can inform our journey.

On the other hand, we also need to bear in mind that the entrepreneurial context and challenges are distinct in some ways. Typically, entrepreneurs work in much smaller teams than regular employees of organizations, or even alone. Therefore, they might be prone to feelings of isolation and exposed to phases of even more intense work. After all, if they don't get it done, nobody will and they directly have to deal with the effects of such failure. In organizational settings, the chances are higher that someone can take over without the business immediately stopping to run. Furthermore, depending on the stage of their venture, entrepreneurs have to continuously learn new skills to meet the emerging challenges of new ventures. These skills potentially also involve tasks related to innovation, which by definition involve more ambiguity and uncertainty than, for example, routine tasks in marketing or production. Lastly, entrepreneurs might benefit from the fact that they are their own boss. If they have the right tools and awareness, they have more autonomy to take care of their tasks and own well-being. Furthermore, they will ideally be pursuing a vision that is led by a purpose that is important to them. This should make their activities more fulfilling in their own right. So, while we can learn from previous initiatives and research in the workplace and leadership context, we should not assume that it is directly transferable to the everyday life of entrepreneurs. Ultimately, more scientific research is needed to fully understand mindfulness in the entrepreneurial context. With that in mind, let's look at some previous insights and underlying mechanisms.

## Mindfulness at Work

In the last section, I mentioned the review of studies on mindfulness in the workplace of Darren Good and other researchers. Since the study is quite new, very comprehensive and well cited in the academic world, it is a good place to start considering the underlying mechanisms of mindfulness in workplace settings. Good and colleagues suggest that increasing evidence across multiple fields suggests a fundamental connection of mindfulness to many aspects of workplace functioning as well as well-being. Consequently, they make an effort to review research into how mindfulness influences human attention, with follow-up effects on functional aspects like *cognition*, *emotion*, *behavior* and *physiology*. Most interestingly, the authors report consequent impact on key workplace outcomes, including performance, relationships, and well-being. As summarized in Figure 11, the study summarizes positive effects of mindfulness as a personality trait or mindfulness practice on important aspects, like:

- Stress reduction
- Teamwork and relationships in the workplace
- Communication
- Job and task performance
- Physical and psychological well-being
- Leadership

They even suggest mindfulness as a fundamentally new principle to guide research in future organi-

| MINDFULNESS | | | |
|---|---|---|---|
| Trait | State | Practice | Intervention |

⌄

**HUMAN FUNCTIONING**

| ATTENTION | | |
|---|---|---|
| Stability | Control | Efficiency |

| COGNITION | EMOTION | BEHAVIOR | PHYSIOLOGY |
|---|---|---|---|
| Capacity, flexibility | Life cycle, reactiviy, tone | Self-regulation, reduced automaticity | Stress response, neuroplasticity, aging |

⌄

**WORKPLACE OUTCOMES**

| PERFORMANCE | RELATIONSHIPS | WELL-BEING |
|---|---|---|
| Job, task, etc. | Leadership, teamwork, etc. | Psychological, physical, etc. |

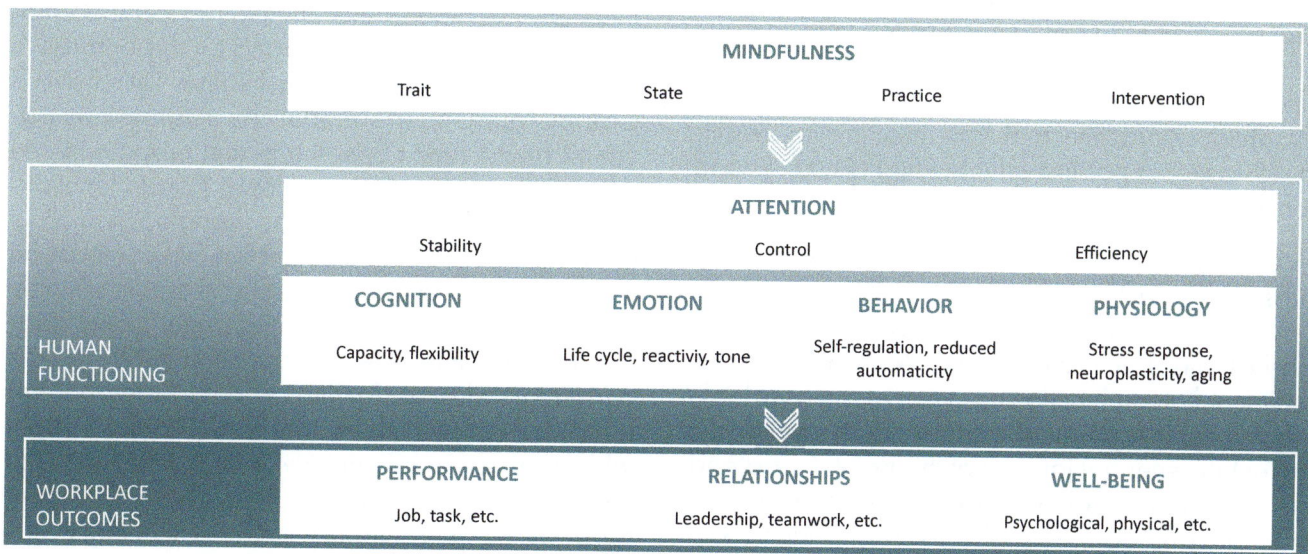

*Figure 11: Mechanisms and effects of mindfulness in the workplace. Adapted from Good et al. (2016). With kind permission from Sage Publications.*

zational research. Therefore, the assumption that mindfulness-based interventions are beneficial in the context of entrepreneurship is strengthened. So, what are the mechanisms Good and colleagues discovered? They discuss how mindfulness affects several domains of human functioning and consequently leads to the positive outcomes listed before. They suggest *attention, cognition, emotion, behavior* and *physiology* as important mediators between mindfulness as a *personality trait, temporal state, practice* or *intervention* and key workplace outcomes. If you are interested in the current understanding how improved *stability, control* and *efficiency* of attention can be cultivated with mindfulness practice and how this, in turn, results in downstream positive effects, I highly recommend reading the review.

In Chapter 5, we discussed the idea that mindfulness might positively affect several functional aspects of the entrepreneurial journey. Now, I want to address this issue in more detail. While all of the domains of human functioning deserve a closer look, we will get into detail about the role of *emotions* in the entrepreneurial journey at this point. Good and his colleagues provide an excellent overview of emotions and of how mindfulness might help to regulate them to find more balance in a stressful work environment. They build on Nico Frijda's definition of emotions.[27] In simple terms, emotions are the internal reactions to events we experience and they stimulate subsequent behavior. According to Good and colleagues, mindfulness influences emotions through attentional *stability, control* and *efficiency*. Being more conscious about the stimuli we observe also alters how they are evaluated and how they are manifested in our emotional reactions. However, I believe that simply being aware of emotional

reactions is not the end of the story. More important is the question of how to actually handle difficult emotional environments, such as the conditions of extreme uncertainty in startups. That's where compassion comes into play.

## Compassion and Entrepreneurship

The last chapter concluded with a journaling exercise. I did not randomly choose the three domains I asked you to journal on. In the end, this was a first exercise in guiding your attention to certain emotional patterns. I want to expand on this before we get into our Deep Dive with Hanna. Let's have a look at Paul Gilbert's model. As illustrated in Figure 12 on the next page, the model proposes three major affect regulation systems in human functioning.[28] In his book *The Compassionate Mind*, Paul Gilbert takes a scientific deep dive into compassion and describes several mechanisms that are highly relevant to the context of entrepreneurs and startups. His main line of reasoning is that our brains still carry many desires, feelings and fantasies that are a result of our evolutionary history. While we might tell ourselves to be entirely evolved beings, that version might not always be the entire truth. Gilbert suggests that we still carry some evolutionary heritage. We still share common basic emotions and the way they are triggered with many animals. Anger, anxiety and pleasure guide us through life and motivate our actions, just as they guide our closer or more distant relatives in the animal kingdom. Often we are not strongly aware of these emotions. Indeed, we are hard on ourselves for feeling them and letting our actions be guided by them. Here, Paul Gilbert suggests that mindfulness practice is just the right tool to use on the awareness part. In a simplified view, these emotions are represented by three major affect regulation systems.

They work independently and balance each other in a complex interdependence, which goes beyond this discussion. Hence, we will stick to Gilbert's straightforward model. Most interesting for us is probably the *drive system*. Generally speaking, it is a system that creates positive feelings to motivate us to seek resources for survival and prosperity. Doesn't seem too irrelevant to what entrepreneurs do, right? We are deep down the rabbit whole of goal-directed behavior and hence, *striving*! As a reaction to positive life events, our brain rewards us with positive feelings through substances, such as dopamine. Yet, there is a downside to it. What if things don't turn out as we expected them to? While this system is crucial for our survival, if it is overactive, it might create dependency and consequently even undermine our sense of self-worth. Indeed, Paul Gilbert specifically suggests that people with bipolar disorders can have problems with this system. Remember the study from Chapter 2, which showed that entrepreneurs might have up to an eleven-fold risk of reporting a bipolar disorder during their lifetime?[29] Entrepreneurs are bound to strive for their goals. It is their "raison d'etre". They work hard and channel resources in new directions to create something that does not exist, yet. Often, they do so against obstacles and over long periods of time. However, just like anybody else, they need balance in their emotional experience. This might be a very tough challenge. Yuval Engel beautifully put it this way:

**"What entrepreneurs do is almost a more extreme form of what humans do."**

So, let's look at how that reflects in the other two affect regulation systems in Gilbert's model. If things don't go quite well or we face a serious threat, our *threat system* gets activated. To give a little bit of tribute to this system, it is probably what let our species survive until this point. Its main purpose is protection. Yet, it can't differentiate between more or less serious threats very well. Modern society potentially drives us into too many threat-related responses and can result in detrimental health effects. Burnout anyone? Basically, our body can't really distinguish between an approaching pack of wolves and an important deadline... The amygdala is often discussed as a central structure in these operations and it has quite some autonomy to "overwrite" other emotions in our brain. Entrepreneurial fear of failure is a hot topic in entrepreneurship research and I believe that future research should have a close look at the mechanisms of this system. In one of his studies, Yuval Engel already showed how brief loving-kindness meditations can help entrepreneurs to handle fear of failure.[30]

An important aspect in this study is something that we didn't specifically address so far, compassion. This in turn is closely linked to the last of the three systems, the *soothing system*. Here, I believe we are in the conceptual domain of *being* and the emotional state connected to it. For many, it might be less intuitive to grasp this one. Gilbert suggests that the soothing system helps to restore balance by nurturing feelings of contentment, inner peacefulness and connectedness.[31] This calm sense of well-being can be activated by affection and kindness from other beings, but also by treating ourselves in that manner. A mother calming down her child is a very good example of how this system works.

In that regard, there are some more exciting find-

Driven, excited, vitality

Content, safe, connect

Incentive/
resource-focused

Wanting, pursuing,
achieving, consuming

Activating

Non-wanting/
affiliative-focused

Safeness-kindness

Soothing

Threat-focused

Protection and
safety-seeking

Activating/
inhibiting

Anger, anxiety, disgust

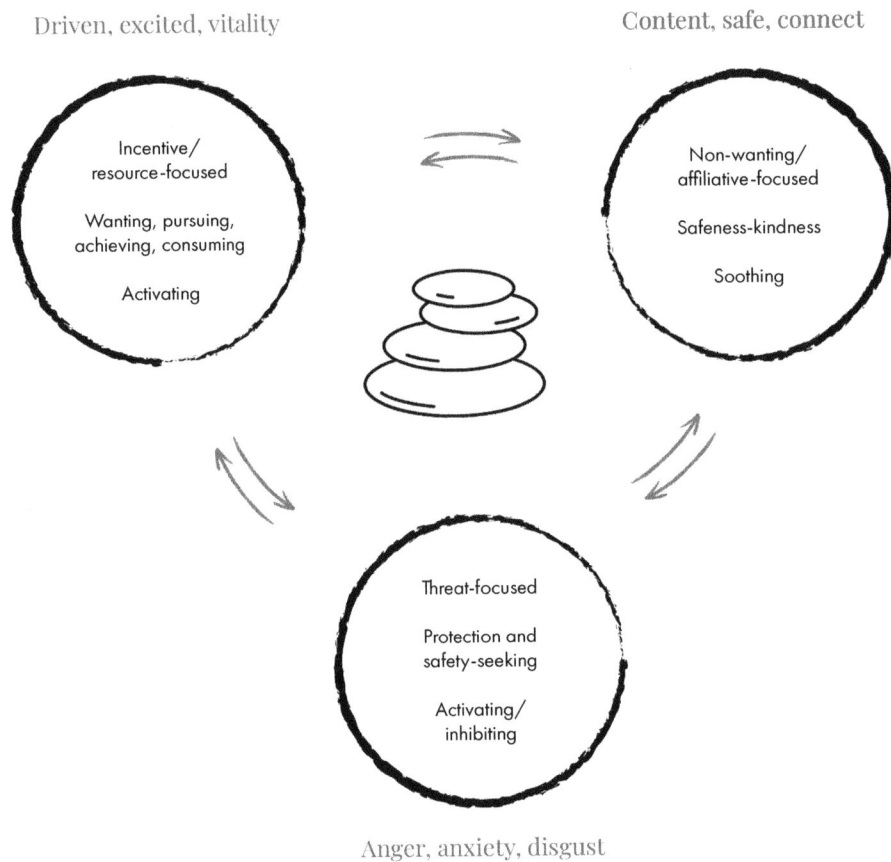

*Figure 12: Three types of affect regulation system.*
*Adapted from Paul Gilbert (2009). The Compassionate Mind.*
*With kind permission from Paul Gilbert.*

ings. Research shows functional and structural changes in the amygdala and the prefrontal cortex among experienced meditators and participants of MBSR programs.[32] As summarized by a recent review, in various studies with stressed, anxious as well as healthy people, the prefrontal cortex showed more activity, connectivity and increased volume after mindfulness-based interventions. Furthermore, MBSR leads to changes in the amygdala, which are in line with improved abilities of emotion regulation as a result of the program. Additionally, researchers observed decreased functional activity, improved functional connectivity with the prefrontal cortex, and earlier deactivation after experiencing emotional stimuli in the amygdala. So, MBSR-induced emotional and behavioral changes are actually related to changes in the brain and seem closely knit to our emotional experiences. Hence, systematic meditation interventions might play a crucial role for entrepreneurs' emotional balance or *tone*. Another important idea in this regard is cultivating *compassion*, which is the central element of Paul Gilbert's approach to creating emotional balance. Hence, his book title — *The Compassionate Mind*. Compassion is a feeling that arises within us when we witness another beings suffering and we experience a corresponding desire to help.[33] Yet, it can also be directed at oneself, which then is called *self-compassion*.[34] According to Kristin Neff, cultivating self-compassion essentially means becoming kind and understanding towards oneself, getting conscious about our common human experience and developing the ability to mindfully attend to difficult emotions without getting absorbed in them. As Yuval Engel showed, loving-kindness meditation helps to stimulate a self-compassionate attitude and helps to handle difficult entrepreneurial experiences, such as the fear of failure.[35] I believe that compassion and self-compassion are crucially important aspects to guide the entrepreneurial journey and they can be cultivated through meditation, too.

Yet, I suppose that compassion and self-compassion are not a natural part of "the entrepreneurial deal". That might be an important reason for the well-being challenge that many business founders face and an opportunity to create emotional balance. In Chapter 2, Rogelio shared some nice examples, how he became more appreciative of his social, mental and physical needs. After becoming aware of them and learning to feel more connected to himself and his environment, he started treating himself with more compassion. I believe that finding a balance between the emotional systems is also fundamental to the idea of Being-while-Striving. It is not necessarily about *what* we do, but *how* we do it and how that reflects in your emotional experience.

This comes down to the idea of contentment. As changemakers, we are obviously not entirely content with the way things are. Otherwise, we wouldn't want to change them, right? However, being content with the way things are *unfolding* and trusting that we are doing the best job we can, might make a crucial difference in our emotional experience! Paul Gilbert shares a very suitable example in his book.[36] The Dalai Lama is constantly traveling, doing interviews, giving talks, visiting conferences, writing books and finding new ways to spread the idea of compassion in the world. He is obviously *striving* to do so. Yet, he always seems to be at peace with himself and the world around him. Could there be a better example of

Being-while-Striving? Enough of the theory! Let's ask a true expert on the matter. Escaping the busy work environment of a business consultant, Hanna Tempelhagen co-founded The Mindful Spaces in Hamburg. She is a certified MBSR teacher, and guess what... She guided the eight-week MBSR program I took part in. Let's hear her story, how mindfulness and compassion connect and how that might be relevant for mindful startups!

# Deep Dive

A Conversation with Hanna Tempelhagen,
the Courageous Mindfulness and MBSR Teacher

Malte: Hanna, I am happy to learn more about your story today. You are a certified MBSR teacher, you offer MBSR courses and as a co-founder of The Mindful Spaces, you are an entrepreneur yourself! That in itself is an exciting perspective on Entrepreneurial Mindfulness. How did you get here? What is your story?

Hanna: Well, how did I get here... It's indeed a fascinating personal journey that I went through. It is not like I planned to exactly do what I am doing now. When I finished high school and contemplated about my future, to be honest, my expectations were set on a big career. I sent applications to various business schools and indeed accepted an offer of one of them. I started at ESB Reutlingen with a double diploma in international management and French. Then I realized... Well, I dropped out of my studies. That was due to several reasons. On the one hand, I realized what my own internal motivation was. Looking back today, I had a real breakdown. I broke down under my own expectations, my perfectionism and my standards towards myself.

Malte: May I ask, was it your ego that played a major role pushing you into this?

Hanna: Yes, you can say that it was my ego, but it was also defiance. You should know that I grew up in an environment in which music and arts were very important. Money was always a big topic and my idea was certainly not living like this. I didn't want to worry about money anymore. And hence, the idea to pursue a successful corporate career in an international environment, ideally in a German-French company or corporation. French had been my first foreign language and I had followed a bilingual program at high school. Then, I experienced the first time that my body sent me a clear signal. I broke down under my own expectations and the stress of being surrounded by many people that were all under the pressure to constantly perform. I always had this ideal picture of myself being a successful businesswoman, top-performing, always good looking, in perfect shape... I was never satisfied with what I had. This is actually the first time that I share this story in public.

Malte: Thank you so much Hannah; I really appreciate your trust and courage!

Hanna: I then made a decision to stay in a psychosomatic clinic for a while, recover from this phase and decide what I want to do now. This was the one thing I did. The other thing was that I still decided to study business administration, but this time at a public university. I started in Mainz and still had an internal conflict about quitting the business school. For a long time, I maintained my enrollment and considered it as a semester that I took off, due to illness and return later. But I got a lot of influence from home and my social environment and decided ok – I will go for the public university. Which does not imply that I stopped putting myself under pressure. My expectations remained the same. I just went to a public university. To wrap this up, I went to Paris and followed my plan, but I had panic attacks. The reason for this was that I was always a top performer in school and always had the best grades. Then, I had this breakdown at Reutlingen and then, for the first time in my life I failed an exam. This led to panic attacks because my degree was at stake. I went for an exchange semester, failed some attempts and had to pass this damn last exam.

This actually led me to reconsider the way I handled this situation. I had to do something different. These were the first encounters with meditation. Also, in form of autogenous training. Well, I say first encounters because I started autogenous training and found some variations, which helped me to calm down and be more focused. I started reading about these things. That were my first approaches. Through this, I learned to deal better with the pressure of examinations, but essentially, I did not really let go of the high expectations towards myself.

And that also reflected in my first job. I kept up certain patterns that I carried within myself again and again. Even in other situations. The same situation kept up coming up in my life in different contexts and that led to a deeper desire to explore this on a deeper level. I realized that this has nothing to do with the people around me, but with myself. With the way I treated myself and behaved when interacting with other people. This has resulted in more intense involvement with meditation, so-called *active meditations*. At this time, I lived in Berlin and had a similar experience like in Reutlingen. While I previously had a breakdown in context with my studies, I now experienced a breakdown due to my job environment. I took over a very, very big project — and lost it. Whereupon, on a Friday afternoon, I got fired. I was ordered to my managers' office and received the termination of my job contract.

Malte: Wow, that is tough...

Hanna: And without suspecting something! That was a digital transformation project and I put my whole heart into it and I did not even notice that I did so. That was the time for me to really get into these internal processes. And that's what I did! For several years, I practiced dynamic and other active meditations as taught by Osho in parallel to my regular working life. I also did some kind of inner transformational training for several months. Imagine 21 days of meditation, one-hour meditations at 7am, which goes through 5 phases of intense breathing patterns, a space for emotional expression, lettings things go... I don't want to describe all the single phases, but you might say that it is some kind of therapeutic relief. Letting things go through an intense physical process. Yet, it also provides room for silence by intentionally completely stopping all activity at some point and just observe. Observe what is going on in the body and mind. Doing a very dynamic movement and then just stop! Everything freezes. I observe the breathe, the heartbeat, the sweat dripping, I observe that it also gets intense to just remain in this position for 15 minutes. Realizing how the wish to change something emerges. And this practice happens through several cycles. I then also did a teacher training with over 360 hours of training, facilitating groups myself and with that experiencing a very, very intense phase of my life. Yet, it opened my own ability to dive deeper into silence.

During that time, to add the entrepreneurial perspective, I started a business in the area of digital business development and consulting. I had smaller customers and solopreneurs, mid-size companies, but also big corporations. That is something I still did in the context of business consulting. So, this part did not entirely disappear. I worked in consulting several times and even though I made certain experiences during my meditation practice, I always ended it up in these vicious circles. Because, if you work in the service sector, you have these *deadlines* and you have to stick to them! And of course, sometimes you understand things differently. Communication has a big influence on that and it may happen that you work towards something that was intended in a completely different way. Then, you have to rework everything and you work until late at night. Long story short, I did this as an entrepreneur and started a business in the digital business consulting sector and strategic consulting. In parallel, I focused more and more on the mindfulness part. I started including meditations and mindfulness aspects. I had this phase in which I decided to go for the relatively more relaxed option of employment. For about two years, I worked for an agency in a management position for online marketing. I used to integrate meditations and similar approaches for my team. During that time, I also started to become more open towards MBSR. More open in the sense that I started looking for something with a scientific foundation. So, something that provides scientific evidence on the effects of meditation and why they occur.

Malte: So, to understand the mechanisms behind the scenes?

Hanna: Right! And that's how I got to hear about MBSR. I also took part in a course in the Charité hospital in Berlin. They offer courses with several MBSR trainers. It was immediately clear to me that I will do the license training. Now, we get closer to the point when I met my co-founder Michael Merks in the context of coaching. The idea to put humans first started to emerge. That is something he always did. Around that time, several people had the idea to found The Mindful Spaces. That was a point when I sort of gravitated into this venture. I was not involved right from the beginning, but I joined the conversation quite quickly. For Michael and me it became clear that we wanted to establish it in a more formal way and found a GmbH. That is the actual time of starting up. I kind of got you the whole story now...

Malte: Well, the story is so exciting! Thank you so much for sharing it. When I started this journey into Entrepreneurial Mindfulness, I never expected to hear such personal experiences. Sure, I am interested in the expert perspectives but these personal stories really bring things to life. I think this was really beautiful and fascinating. I could go on and ask about so many things, but I am curious about a very particular viewpoint of yours. And with your personal story in mind, I am now very much looking forward to your answer. If we talk about mindfulness in the workplace and mindful leadership, an eight-week program, like MBSR is probably not too feasible. However, you said yourself that you are interested in MBSR because it is backed by so much scientific work. In your opinion, what is absolutely essential for, potentially shorter programs, in other contexts? What would have to be included to ensure the effectiveness of such a program?

Hanna: From my point of view, the most important things are, and that's independent of the duration of practice or the type of program, twofold. The first one is an openness and voluntary participation of the persons involved. It should not become the next "to-do"! Additionally, there should be a strong management commitment on a very high level. Up to the executive board. I made experiences, also in startups, where on the management level everything was perfect because there was high commitment. However, it was not communicated authentically. To be precise, when I start such a program and on the first day the person who should be a role model does not participate with the excuse of having a call, that basically undermines the entire endeavor. With this statement, authentically getting across the point of such a program will be really hard. So, to get back to your question, the commitment from management or founders to be open-minded, really engage in the program and then walk the talk as a role model. Even if it is a new thing for me, I should be curious and not sit in the session with a smartphone in my hands. What does it represent if I make an exception for myself because I am so busy and have so many meetings? As a leader, I am a role model. For me, these are the points that have to be clear before talking about the duration and setting of the program. If we talk about my idea of an ideal setting, I have various experiences. For example, one or two-day workshops, because there is quite some demand for this format. This can work if it is repeated on a regular basis, but continuity is key. If we look at some HR departments, it is sometimes considered a trend that has to be followed.

Malte: So, it is again just another item on their "to-do list"?

Hanna: Right, and at the end of the day, this is not really sustainable. That is why I believe in a certain structure. I like to do an introduction where I provide a certain basis and some scientific fundamentals. However, this should not be done in a classic PowerPoint presentation setting.

Malte: So, you don't just want to repeat the facts and overwhelm everybody with an information overload?

Hanna: Well, I discuss the facts – showing the benefits and why it works, but then I want to make it experiential in nature and include exercises for everything. This way, there's always a reflection of – what did I experience? Additionally, there should be regular sessions during a longer period of time. Not necessarily two and a half hours, like in MBSR though. That is usually not really feasible in a corporate context. At least, and maybe that is my own prejudice, it is currently not realistic. Regarding the specific exercises, there are studies that show 20 minutes of regular practice already show positive effects on the body, stress response or hormone balance. Therefore, my program is based on this introductory session and a respective regular program over a certain period.

During the Corona pandemic, I actually do this in a digital setting and I see that is possible. We have developed a two-day workshop format with a six-week guided follow-up. Still, most of the corporate programs we do at The Mindful Spaces, are very individual with respect to the specific organizational context and we intentionally do this. We know almost all the programs in the market, such as "Search Inside Yourself (by Google)" or "Mindful Leadership" by Janice Marturano, SAM and so on... I personally completed a training for "Mindfulness at The Workplace", which is it quite intense with regard to the single session and is a 10-week program. Yet, it also leaves certain flexibility. Long story short, such a program for at the workplace has to allow the integration into personal work routines and a work environment, which enables that. The work environment is not limited to the physical space. Of course, it is nice to have this and *new work* has a point. A pleasant work experience and an according workstation is a part of *new work*, but there is more to it. I can easily do this at my regular desk. That is if I bring the right attitude into it and if my team and my boss create the right atmosphere.

Malte: Ok. I think I understand what you mean. Basically, I have to know that nobody looks at me in a strange way when I sit at my desk and meditate, right?

Hanna: Voilà! If there is a shared commitment to appreciate the own energy level and say – yes, now I do my three-minute breathing exercise. Or maybe, you even integrate it into the teamwork or take a 20-minute bodyscan practice on the mat. Furthermore, there are some programs that include a train the trainer approach within the organization and we get some requests for that. Training mindfulness ambassadors, if you like. The rationale is to amplify the process of spreading mindfulness within the company. I do like the idea, but I must say that so far, organizations want a fast-forward program. Mindfulness is not something that I can swallow in a magic pill.

The details are very important when I guide meditations. The words that I use and how I use them, that has implications on the experience of the participants. And I can trigger a lot of things with my words. If I am not aware of that or I do not guide based on my own experience, my experience is that it has other effects. This also reflects in the feedback of many participants. Reactions range from easily tuning into the instructions to strong rejections. This is my perspective as somebody with an intense training and education over many years. Also, with regard to knowing what I experienced myself and an awareness of how long it took me. I must say, and I consciously make a judgment here, that this is a personal quality expectation from myself. This is the one side of it, but there is also a responsibility I have towards fellow human beings. As I said, I can cause many things that are not just a pleasant experience. I have to be constantly aware of that. Therefore, such an organizational ambassador approach requires well-grounded training. Simply learning meditations by heart or reading them aloud is certainly not a solution. It is an inner development process and I need to know what happens during this process.

Malte: That makes a lot of sense to me... Thank you. That was very insightful! So, I hear that yes — people in startups and organizations have limited time, but at the end of the day mindfulness is about taking time for yourself. This can be done in different ways, but there is no shortcut. As you said, you can't swallow it in a magic pill. Such a program might just be the first step in bringing mindfulness into people's lives and it may motivate them to continue on the journey. Yet, even igniting this spark requires time, calmness and commitment.

Hanna: Yes, and openness from the organization or the founder.

Malte: Right, that was your first point! Ok, I think I have a better understanding of your perspective now.

Hanna, I would like to get to the next topic. Right at the beginning of our conversation, you said that you are very interested in the mechanisms underlying mindfulness and its positive effects. I am totally with you in that regard. Yet, it is such a complex topic and I am impressed by all the internal effects, psychological mechanisms and so on. One particular aspect that you shared on your Instagram recently sparked my interest. I am talking about Gilbert's three system model of affect regulation. The reason for this is best explained by a quote of Yuval Engel from my last conversation — "Being an entrepreneur is a more extreme kind of being human." Yes, we all have our drive and our motivation, but entrepreneurs' purpose of existence is basically to act with the future in mind. It is their own endeavor and personal successes might even be addictive. For example, I read in a recent study that entrepreneurs are much more likely to report bipolar disorder during their lifetime. I am curious if a meditation training for entrepreneurs could benefit from Gilbert's perspective. Creating balance by getting out of this pure *striving* mode. What is your take on that?

Hanna: Certainly, emotional regulation and dealing with our emotions is an important topic, which is captured in Gilbert's model. In that context, *compassion* is a very important perspective. Being compassionate and self-compassionate is something I did not explicitly mention, yet. Personally, I believe that mindfulness should include these aspects. However, they are often considered distinct things. This implies being compassionate and especially compassionate towards myself, accepting myself and treating myself with loving kindness when things might not turn out the way I expected them to. Especially as an entrepreneur, there are so many ups and downs. You have your successes and they are great and you want more of that, but how do you deal with obstacles like an investor dropping out? How do I treat myself? Do I tell myself things like — "I knew it!", "You should have been better!" and so on? Of course, your inner *drive* is very important as an entrepreneur. What drives me? What is my passion? However, you need to create a balance and respect that you are a human being. It is ok to appreciate myself, love myself and treat myself with loving-kindness when things don't work out. I believe that many entrepreneurs would greatly benefit from that. I can also say that from my own experience. One of the largest studies on how different forms of meditation affect our behavior and stress regulation is a study by the Max Planck Institute in Leipzig by Tanja Singer.

Malte, I feel my concentration is not where I would like it to be. Would you mind a moment of silence?

Malte: Let's walk the talk!

*We meditate for a moment*

Hanna: Ok! So, one of the biggest findings of the study was that loving-kindness meditations had indeed stronger effects on stress response on a physiological level than for example, breathing meditations and body scans. Another practice is sharing feelings of compassion in one-on-one conversations, which also had positive effects. So, compassion has certain effects that are distinct from other approaches to meditation. If we take self-compassion into consideration, Kristin Neff and Christoph Germer have done great work on this and conducted several studies. My co-founder Michael Merks is also specialized in compassion and self-compassion. Regarding the question, if something that takes Gilbert's three systems of affect regulation into consideration should be integrated into a program for Entrepreneurs, I would say that this is a clear *yes!* Definitely, such elements should be included in programs. Also, when we talk about the leadership context. I am usually a role model and how do I treat myself in that position? Am I hard on myself and punish myself for not being good enough or do I treat myself in a compassionate way? This is something that my team will be aware of. So, definitely a big plus for integrating compassion and self-compassion elements.

Malte: Cool! I particularly liked that you pointed out the distinction of mindfulness and compassion. Are we talking about simply getting aware of things in a mindful way or are we talking about the consequent reactions to that? That was very insightful for me and clarifies how compassion and self-compassion relate to mindfulness and can be applied to consciously guide behavioral changes.

Hanna: Well, if you read about mindfulness and why you should care about it, better concentration, less mind-wandering, being more energetic and more creativity are common arguments. These are the hard facts, if you would like to call it that. Curiously, the entrepreneurs I currently do trainings with mention these exact points. I want to be more focused, I want to be more present and not zone out all the time and so on. The other component, which is clearly a part of mindfulness in a more Buddhist sense, is acting from your heart. So, mindfulness is *heartfulness!* Yet, this component is often left out of the picture. Depending on whom you ask, people might say compassion and self-compassion are an integral part of mindfulness. Sure, I need the attention to what is happening in the present moment. For example, when I am not feeling good or let's just stay with disappointment. First of all, getting aware of this and then considering what I can do for myself. Going into the next layer is developing a feeling for the things that I need to get better or maybe just being able to be with that feeling. And then, getting aware of the fact that in this present moment there are many more who exactly feel like me right now is the third component.

Malte: Beautiful! I think it is a very important point to appreciate this scientific approach to mindfulness has enabled to reduce its complexity and enable scientific research. Yet, in its original tradition it is much richer and aspects like self-compassion and compassion are an integral part of it. We should not forget that! I feel that this is quite a nice thought to proceed to the end of this conversation. I have one more question for you, Hanna. Feel free to express your very own opinion for this one. If you hear "creating the future from the present moment" what does this mean for you and how does it resonate with you?

Hanna: Allow me to just be with this for a while!

Malte: Sure thing.

*Another minute of silence*

Hanna: Initially, I got aware of this inner dialogue with myself. How should this be possible? So, a very critical question. If I am here in this moment, how can I open up for something that happens at some point in the future? There was this inner voice, which told me that it is about this present moment. The past is the past and the future is the future. How can I create the future from the present moment? And the other voice, which is coming up while I speak it right now, says a very different thing. Yes, this is in my hands right now! In this very moment, it is in my own hands how my actions or non-actions affect my future and the future of others. This is the one thing. In the sense that I am conscious about my own responsibilities as a human being, as a living being and as an entrepreneur. What is my purpose? What is driving me? What resonates with me and how do I affect the future of our planet with my actions? It opens up the possibility of being in this present moment and envisioning how it could be. Even though I use this moment with all my awareness to get a glimpse of the future. Yet, it happens from the moment and it happens with my entire consciousness. It is a conscious glimpse into the future and not an unconscious one! When I allow myself to fully be in that vision of how our future could be and the awareness that my actions of today can have an influence on this future, this will again influence my present moment actions. That is what it means to me.

Malte: Wow! Thank you... I believe that it seems like a paradox indeed. Yet, it is the paradox that has to be untangled if we want to empower changemakers who want to mindfully create the future. I really love your answer and I don't have anything to add to that! Thank you for your insights and the inspiration.

Hanna: Yes, I really feel that through speaking this out loudly, I found a certain truth for myself.

## In a Nutshell...

Developing an entrepreneurial mindset and getting through the entrepreneurial journey is supported by various institutions with a variety of activities. While universities often enlighten a spark and teach relevant approaches, accelerators and incubators are much more utility-based in nature. They are about getting stuff done. Accordingly, the mental support needs of nascent and actual entrepreneurs vary. In the last chapter, I envisioned an Entrepreneurial Mindfulness Training Program for the educational context. Yet, entrepreneurs in action are usually more experienced on the practical side of things and might need more condensed approaches. Mindfulness at work programs provide rich ground to provide such support. However, entrepreneurs deal with unique challenges and mindfulness-based programs should consider this. Research suggests that mindfulness-based training programs are increasingly applied in work settings, which usually involve shorter versions of well-researched programs (for example, MBSR). These training programs can indeed be transferred to specific contexts, such as entrepreneurship. Coupling mindfulness with other training can produce beneficial synergistic effects, but requires careful consideration and including the knowledge and advice of experts, like Hanna.[37]

However, we learned from Hanna that an *openness* towards mindfulness and compassion as well as a commitment to bringing it into everyday business is crucial for founders and founding teams. Besides any support from the outside, for example in the form of adapted mindfulness at work programs, this has to begin in the founding team itself. Hence, *The Mindful Startup*. This reminds me of my own PhD research on the right mindset for innovation and entrepreneurship.[38] Maybe, entrepreneurs, startups and businesses need to develop a *mindfulness mindset* in the first place. Having a glance at the entrepreneurial mindset definition, I propose that:

**A mindfulness mindset is a willingness and ability to sense and realize the opportunities of integrating mindfulness-based approaches into one's own life and an organizational context.**

On the content side of things, a full-day kick-off provides a basis to get relevant knowledge across and create some first experiences. While it might not be an eight-week program, continuity is still key and "mindfulness cannot be swallowed in a magic pill". Several reoccurring sessions of at least 20 minutes are still necessary and should be a part of programs focused on experienced entrepreneurs. Lastly, compassion and self-compassion emerge as a valuable addition to the cultivation of mindfulness and it might well be a secret power for stressed-out entrepreneurs. In that sense, compassion might be a way to balance "the dark side of passion".[39] Paul Gilbert's model of affect regulation provides a hands-on tool for self-reflection and getting aware of emotional imbalances. Let's turn our hearts and minds towards compassion! We heard that it is traditionally a part of Buddhist practice and I feel that it brings a lot more "soul" into our journey. In the last chapter, I asked you to journal about your three affect regulation systems. Now, we will build on that!

# I Dare You:

## Become Self-Compassionate!

- Get a blank sheet of paper and a pen
- Start with a minute of silence and fully arrive in the moment wherever you are right now
- Based on the journaling exercise from last chapter, recap the three emotional drive systems and how they manifest in your life
  - How often are you in your *drive system*?
  - How often do you get into your *threat protection system*?
  - How often are you in your *soothing system*?
- Draw a circle for each system with a size according to how present they are in your life
- Stay with the picture you get for a while and ask yourself if it represents the balance you need and feel is sustainable for your life
- Maybe it is time for the loving-kindness meditation from Chapter 5?
  - Remind yourself that you are doing the best that you can
  - Remind yourself that we are all in this together and you are not alone with your struggles
- Allow yourself to be content with the way things are unfolding
- Take self-responsibility, speak out an intention to compassionately take care of your own well-being and create enough space to get into your *soothing system*

"The powers of science and technology now have to be matched by the inner developments of humanity."

JACK KORNFIELD, NO TIME LIKE THE PRESENT

# 09 Mindful Innovation Ecosystems

What if we took the idea of Entrepreneurial Mindfulness even further? What if entire *innovation ecosystems* were designed to promote mindful change and educate mindful changemakers? At the beginning of Chapter 7, we saw that innovation ecosystems, such as those of universities, play a crucial role in honing the entrepreneurial mindset. In this chapter, we will conduct a thought experiment around one of the most vibrant innovation ecosystems I know, the University of Twente! Another fact makes this ecosystem very interesting for our thought experiment. The University of Twente deliberatively designed human-centeredness into its approach to innovation and entrepreneurship. Yet, *human-centered innovation* usually refers to a process of innovation, which is closely aligned to uncovering user needs and thus, providing better solutions to people's actual problems. What if we created an environment, which directs the human-centeredness of driving change at beneficiaries as well as facilitators of innovation? An innovation ecosystem that fosters mindfulness and compassion. The DesignLab in Twente is a central institution of the university's innovation ecosystem and provides fertile soil for this idea. Of course, we will not leave it at a thought experiment! At the end of this chapter, we will challenge these ideas in a Deep Dive with Miriam Iliohan who is a co-founder and manager of the DesignLab. Before we can do that, we need to have a closer look at the concept of innovation ecosystems, the DesignLab and human-centered innovation.

## Innovation Ecosystems

According to Granstrand and Holgersson, Innovation ecosystems are complex systems and on a more abstract level, they build on three main components.[40] First, ecosystems require human beings to engage in innovative activities and support each other. These *actors* of an ecosystem could be mentors, workshop facilitators, inspired students, citizens or employees. In many environments, innovation is not a formal part of people's contract or social contract. They need to be inspired or motivated with incentives. Remember the Deep Dive with Dagmar? She suggested that the willingness part of an entrepreneurial mindset is not even that hard to stimulate. Nevertheless, you do need people to constantly ignite this spark and remove barriers to innovation, because maintaining the *volition* to drive change is a bit of a different story. Second, *actors* need a shared understanding of *activities* that are conductive to driving change collaboratively. Driving sustainable change is a complex endeavor and a shared understanding how to reduce this complexity is crucial to tackle the right problem with the right solution. An increasingly applied approach to coordinate creative teams in developing innovative products and services is design thinking, which I will introduce in more detail in the next section. Third, *artifacts* provide *actors* crucial means to conduct innovative *activities*. Think about maker spaces, which provide changemakers with important machinery for rapid prototyping across the globe or co-working spaces that facilitate collaboration. Yet, it could also be as simple as a whiteboard and some sticky notes. Many people would be surprised how little equipment you actually need to brainstorm the wildest ideas with the right bunch of people and some colorful pieces of paper. Launching an actual product is a completely different story, of course. In combination, *actors*, *activities* and *artifacts* should complement one another and empower a wider population of changemakers to develop, test and implement ideas! Ideally, ideas that can be launched and scaled in viable ventures.

If we look at university innovation systems in particular, we find that many universities today centralize and coordinate educational programs, activities and resources related to entrepreneurship with centers for entrepreneurship.[41] They establish maker spaces to provide changemakers with a physical room to be creative, meet and mentor each other.[42] Or they run incubators and accelerators to help shaping business ideas and provide specialized support services along the entrepreneurial journey.[43] Now that we know the basics, let's make things a little bit more specific! The University of Twente managed to create a truly dynamic innovation ecosystem and became a hotspot for entrepreneurship in Europe with around 50 student startup launches, such as booking.com per year.[44] A central institution in its innovation ecosystem is the DesignLab and its guiding principle is:

### "Connecting Science and Society through Design"[45]

By grounding its approach in the principles and practices of design thinking, it is inherently human-centered already. Let's see how it lives up to that ideal and how such an environment could be infused with mindfulness and compassion!

## Human-Centered Innovation at DesignLab

The DesignLab is a collaborative ecosystem, which strives to empower innovative changemakers.[46] Based on the principles of design thinking it facilitates research, education collaboration and events aiming at creating societal impact.[47] By connecting the University of Twente's ecosystem with citizens and governments, it plays an important role in the "front end of innovation". Thus, it is often the birthplace of ideas, which will then turn into companies and many students' first touchpoint with innovation and entrepreneurship. Before we look at how exactly they do it, we need to do a little crash course on design thinking. Design thinking is a human-centered innovation methodology that embeds a designer's approach to understanding human needs and the facilitating role of technology in a viable business model.[48] It can be thought of as a human-centered and creative mindset, a multidisciplinary toolbox and a process.[49] Let's have a closer look at the process and how it facilitates human-centered problem-solving in multidisciplinary teamwork. Your favorite search engine will show countless design thinking process models, which shows the widespread interest in this approach. Since I collaborate with Stanford's d.school as a Faculty Innovation Fellows candidate, I will present the d.school's process and approach.[50]

Just the right approach for the compassionate entrepreneur, every design thinking process starts with love! If an innovation, in form of a product, service or entirely new business model is supposed to offer actual value, it needs to serve a real human need. By definition, this distinguishes an innovation from an invention. But how do you make sure to do

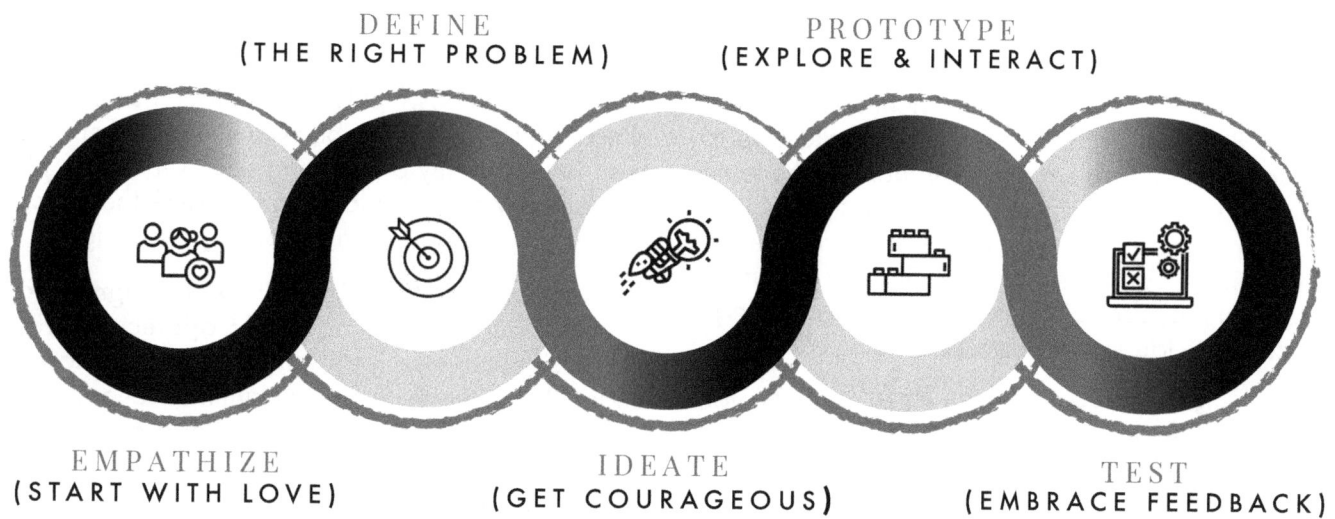

DEFINE
(THE RIGHT PROBLEM)

PROTOTYPE
(EXPLORE & INTERACT)

EMPATHIZE
(START WITH LOVE)

IDEATE
(GET COURAGEOUS)

TEST
(EMBRACE FEEDBACK)

*Figure 13: Design thinking process based on the approach of Stanford University's d.school.*

so? Whatever issue you are trying to tackle, make sure to have a close look at the behavior of real humans in their actual environment. Even better, interact with them and make sure to understand what they think and feel! Explore your inner child and always dig a bit deeper by asking – "why?" Design thinking draws on ethnographic tools, such as observations, shadowing, design probes and diaries. After all, users might not even be aware of their needs and design thinkers set out to reveal that *tacit knowledge*. It's crucial that everybody involved in developing solutions in later process steps truly understands these rich *user insights*. Be visual! Drawings, photos, videos and personas are great tools to condense insights and make them sharable in a team. Building on this, you want to make sure to solve the right problem and everybody in the team has the same understanding of that very problem. Formulate a *point of view*, agree on it with the entire team as your design vision. This key statement does not propose solutions but defines a challenge to generate ideas, which is what you will do next.

Ideation is a process of "going wide". Ideally, you will even "go wild"! There will be more than enough chances to get more realistic along the road. If you shoot for the stars, you'll probably land on the moon. If you shoot for the moon, well... Also, committing to rules like deferring judgment, building on the ideas of others and staying focused on the topic helps a great deal to open the solution space. However, make sure you don't stay in your head while developing creative solutions. No, this time I'm not talking about meditation. Think with your hands, think with your body and act out use cases, think with pen and paper. Prototypes can have many forms and they help you to reveal design assumptions, communicate your vision and facilitate interaction. Finally, you want to test your prototype and learn more about your user as well as your solution. Do so with a *beginner's mindset* and don't try to convince anyone of your solution. This is your chance to refine your idea! Most importantly, don't be shy to jump back in the process and gather new user insights, redefine your problem or ideate again. This applies to the entire process of design thinking, by the way. It is iterative, collaborative and should be fun! If you jump back to Chapter 2 and the purpose-driven business model canvas, design thinking is your process to come up with a meaningful value proposition. Or "the right it" as Alberto Savoia, *pretotyping* lecturer at Stanford University, famously puts it.[51] Fun fact, I sent some digital pretotypes of this book to him on LinkedIn to get his view on my pretotyping skills. Of course, his book is now proudly placed on my desk (he is also a very smart salesperson). I hope I got "it" right...

Anyway, with this brief idea of what design thinking is about, we can now fully appreciate why the DesignLab is such an amazing place! I had a chance to join a track of their summer school as a mentor in 2019, where I gave a Yoga and meditation class. The vivid environment and how innovation just seems to permeate every corner of this place blew my mind. Indeed, it *actually* permeates every corner of the building. The DesignLab offers multipurpose rooms for every activity that gets you through a human-centered innovation process. It provides spaces for meeting with users, clients and stakeholders. From there, you can take ideas forward in group spaces for conceptual work and dedicated brainstorming areas. Workshops for woodwork, electronics and multimedia allow changemakers to explore, refine and communicate their change vision. Dedicated presentation spaces allow to gather crucial feedback or pitch finalized solutions. Almost equally important, a team of students as well as staff mentors and supports the projects and keeps the ideas flowing! To me, this feels like just the right place to create the future from the present moment.

## Mindful Innovation Ecosystems

Then, how could infusing mindfulness into such a thriving ecosystem look like? Arguably, on the entrepreneurial side of things, the DesignLab and its surrounding institutions provide a suitable environment. Entrepreneurs and innovators get ignited to proactively drive change! Yet, how can such ecosystems make sure that the societal component of their mission is deeply rooted in the hearts and minds of their changemakers? Moreover, how can they make sure to ignite them and not to set them on fire, which might end up in an entrepreneurial burnout? I hope that I painted a little picture of the fertile soil of institutions like the DesignLab. Now, let's take this and imagine how *actors*, *activities* and *artifacts* in such an environment could nudge people to integrate mindfulness in their everyday changemaker's life and stimulate a *mindfulness mindset* in the long run. After all, mindfulness at work scholars suggests that traditional mindfulness environments, like monasteries, have very specific cultures, aesthetics and physical spaces to support mindful states.[52] What can organizations learn from these environments?

Let's start with the *actors*. We are social beings and whether we are aware of it or not, our behavior is shaped by the people that surround us. We discussed this concerning the influence of subjective norms on our intentions in Chapter 4. What if mentors in innovation ecosystems are not just trained to stimulate an *entrepreneurial mindset* but to advocate a *mindfulness mindset*, too? Yuval and Hanna already shared examples on how mindfulness finds its way into university and workplace environments. Yet, Rogelio told us that it was never part of his entrepreneurial training. I believe there is much more that educators, trainers and experienced entrepreneurs can do! So-called "FuckUp Nights" are an established format in the entrepreneurial world in which entrepreneurs share their startup failures. What about matching this with "LiftUp Nights" in which experienced entrepreneurs share stories of how they got through the emotional struggles of their entrepreneurial journey? If Brené Brown would read Rogelio's and Hanna's story, I bet she would agree with me that they were both "daring greatly"![53] They took a big leap of vulnerability and shared their own personal struggles. This is an opportunity for future changemakers to get aware of the early signs of giving too much and potential ways out of it.

Such formats already point us into the direction of shared *activities*. What if meditation, compassion and mindfulness practice would become an integral part of entrepreneurial education? Just like design thinking, business model canvases and customer journeys. As discussed in Chapter 7, 93% of MIT Sloan's entrepreneurial self-awareness program participants felt that self-awareness practice can help entrepreneurs create more successful businesses.[54] Therefore, it might be even more important to entrepreneurial success than we think and not only a matter of well-being and pro-social orientation.

Lastly, there are *artifacts*, which for me clearly include the spaces that we create around us. As a student of Yoga, I certainly appreciate the calming and grounding atmosphere of Yoga studios and retreat spaces. In fact, I try to keep my private space similarly simplistic and supportive of mindful daily routines. My meditation cushion is placed prominently at a place where I always see it, there is no TV in my living room, everything has a place and is (mostly) at its place and colors and lights support a soothing atmosphere. Sure, there is probably an entire book to write about these things. The important point is to intentionally create these spaces and encourage their use. As Hanna suggested in our Deep Dive, the right space for mindfulness is not just a matter of physical objects. For example, Google puts a big emphasis on creating an atmosphere of psychological safety for its teams.[55] The attitudes and behaviors of colleagues and mentors are crucially important and show how all three components of mindful innovation ecosystems need to work together, *actors*, *activities* and *artifacts*. I believe that doing so will create yet unexplored synergies and empower the next generation of changemakers to create the future from the present moment. Let's see what Miriam Iliohan, co-founder and manager of DesignLab thinks about these ideas!

# Deep Dive

A Conversation with Miriam Iliohan,
the Wholehearted Innovation Ecosystem Builder

**Malte:** Miriam, I am so happy that we found time today and can talk about your perspective on integrating mindfulness into innovation ecosystems. To provide a little bit of context, you are a co-founder and manager of the DesignLab, you are running the University Innovation Fellows program at the University of Twente and you support the d.school team in hosting the Faculty Innovation Fellows program. How did you end up doing all these things? What is your "personal narrative"?

**Miriam:** My personal narrative, I think, is that I enjoy being this maker of change and empowering people to be able to do what they feel will make a valuable impact within society! It's more about finding the right set of tools and community that they need. And if I can help them in a certain way in reaching those tools, whether it is the DesignLab, which is a physical space, a connection to research or in finding a deeper purpose for themselves, I really enjoy doing that. And I think that's the same with the University Innovation Fellows. It is about encouraging the students (and staff) to make change on (and off) campus of the University. For the Faculty Innovation Fellows program, here I support and empower faculty at different universities to do the same with their students and it all relates around the same thing. That's what I think!

**Malte:** I remember that in an earlier conversation we had, you told me that there was a lot of work involved in setting all of these things up and getting the DesignLab up and running. But this drive to empower changemakers motivated you to take this decision and do it anyway?

**Miriam:** Yeah, I think from the get-go of setting up the DesignLab it was overwhelming, how am I going to do that? On the one hand, you've got researchers who have this vision of how they want to bring together researchers, society, students and using design as the main thread throughout and on the other hand they have their research agendas. Then, there is this physical space... My thought was how is this space going to help these groups collaborate on the challenges of our time? While we're also developing an approach how we work.

When I came in, the general ideas were there, but not per se how the process is going to go or what tools do we have to do this. So, starting up the DesignLab was an iterative process and it continues to be so. For example, connecting to research you are doing Malte, a lot of times the students also want to look into finding themselves. That is something we explored multiple times. The students would suggest we need to get meditation pods, doing Yoga or getting into the habit of centering ourselves. Because a lot of times, students know what they need to know from their study programs, but DesignLab just adds the next dimension.

That's why after a couple of years we also started the transdisciplinary master's insert. It is a six-month program, which we insert into the master's. This way, students extend their studies for another six months to shape a responsible future. It challenges you to apply what you have learned in a way of working with critical and conceptual thinking and problem-solving. Not just to apply to your education, but with the projects, startups, student teams or student associations. Students want to make themselves a better person not just per se in knowledge, but also being a generally well-rounded individual. In that context, they are interested in mindfulness and social entrepreneurship as well. They might be two different things, but they want to make the world a better place and themselves a grounded and valuable person. These things have shown up and the students actually have found solutions, because they are there for one another.

To give you an example, when students, society and researchers are working in DesignLab, they come in contact with people they usually don't associate with, because of their programs and the way these degrees are organized, the space and the social interaction that takes place. Even now, in Covid times, students are working together on projects with other students from programs and they get these (for them) unusual insights. We get reactions like – "Oh wow, why do you do it this way?" This mix of, gender, age, study, cultural and ethical backgrounds or just how the persons are, makes them think more holistically. We say that it gives them an injection and it triggers them to apply this transdisciplinary way of working.

Getting back to the story about how DesignLab got started, first we said, ok we will work multidisciplinary. But then we realized – "No, it's not just multidisciplinary, it's transdisciplinary." It's about adding in all of the components that you've learned along the way, in a way of working with critical and conceptual thinking, solving challenges for and with citizens.

The societal challenges can be from the government, external partners, institutions, like the TUHH, University Innovation Fellows partners, and even citizens... It doesn't matter, but it is about the challenges that you also see together. So, it has been a very iterative process to set up DesignLab, which has been, for me, a way of always putting the students in a position where they have something to say. It's not just about support staff, the executive board or the management team. It's always about what student empowerment can do! That's why it is kind of a natural flow between DesignLab, the University Innovation Fellows and the Faculty Innovation Fellows program. I really see that as a line within my work from the past five to six years. It has really been about not me making the change or me being the one who makes things work, but more about empowering others and connecting others and making sure that it works for them!

Malte: Wow, it's so interesting to hear how the DesingLab constantly reinvents itself and how it emerged during the last years! I also hear that your personal style of leading this change is not actually leading it, but listening to people and empowering them in turning their ideas into reality. And because you do it that way, there is not a clear direction in that sense where your transformation is heading, but it is constantly evolving?

Miriam: Well, DesignLab has a clear direction of working on responsible design and working together with citizens on citizen science and we want to do it in a transdisciplinary way. But it's not that we want to specifically reach a goal on the horizon and we're going to do everything to reach that because it is an iterative process. If the things that we've learned along the way have shown us that we need to pivot, then we need to pivot, right? The world is changing, students are changing, research is changing, so that could really make it so much of a different story at a certain point in time.

Malte: That seems wise indeed! So, you already brought it up that two of the topics that students really want to take forward is driving social or sustainable change, but also the mindfulness topic. Where are they coming from in that regard and why are they advocating specifically this topic?

Miriam: They are advocating it because they see the need. Not per se always in themselves, but in their colleagues. I think it is difficult for the students or the staff to say – "Ok, I'm doing this for myself." I've noticed that it's really about them seeing the need within others. Or if I look at myself and some conversations I had with my students, especially because we are now calling in through Zoom, it sometimes seems more personal. You kind of get a look into – did he or she really get up this morning, did he or she take some time to do their hair, do they seem to be doing ok? Can you see that they are making eye contact? In the past, they would be coming to DesignLab and they would have to get dressed to get out of the door... But now you can look into their homes and you notice that the conversation goes like: "Have you talked to bob?" "Oh yeah, Bob didn't show up and didn't turn on his camera in the last three meetings." "Have you asked him to turn on his camera?" "Yes, but he said that there was something going on." "Yeah, I did the same thing!" You kind of notice that you need to be more mindful about each other.

Also, some people are bringing it up as a conversation. Don't we need to do something about the well-being of the students? Do we not need to do more about it? The students actually brought it up as a subject that they want to do. Even today I talked to students. You might remember that we have DesignLab University where students teach student skills. Which could be something like 3D printing, laser cutting or Arduino or similar subjects. Now, they even want to give courses on well-being, inclusion, diversity and mindfulness. In the past it has always been – "Ok, we have to do 3D printing or we have to operate CNC machines". So very technical skills they wanted to teach to each other. And now, students articulate – "Can we find someone within the team or outside the team who can help us with the mental well-being?" This is something that is felt strongly by students. Not just with me.

Malte: That's so curious! I am happy to hear that, of course. Well, not happy to hear that there is such a pressing need, but I personally agree that there is a need in general. That's why I'm doing what I'm doing in the first place. It's nice to hear that your students want to do something about it. Cool! So what kind of initiatives are they starting in that direction? You mentioned that they are looking at trainings and organizing sessions?

Miriam: The first initiative was just a simple, let's say, a Yoga or mindfulness type of session. They started it with the Corona lockdown together with one of the staff members who also practices Yoga. It really worked well! I kind of envisioned something like that when we talked about you or your colleague Sandra-Luisa being a part of my team and giving sessions like that. I love the fact that you brought these topics to my mind two years ago. In this case, it was a colleague who also has a Yoga school and is giving Yoga classes herself. She suggested to combine it because she noticed that people really need it. That's how it got started. It was an initiative of one person and the students started joining. They were always a little bit sad that it was usually during their class time. Now, you see that the students want to do it themselves in the evening hours and they are trying to look at one another. The initiative started from them saying that they wanted it and the staff member who did it.

Malte: That's so cool! I'm happy to hear that there is some momentum. During the last weeks and months, I had many conversations like ours, I reviewed studies and tried to understand the mechanisms behind the need that your students discovered. Especially in places where people drive change, which is ambiguous, takes a lot of effort and is often very stressful. I have the feeling that especially people who care for other people sometimes get lost in this cause. That's why I believe it is especially important to integrate practices like Yoga, mindfulness, meditation and spaces where you can show up and meet each other as human beings in such environments.

Miriam: Yeah! Have you seen the pods that they have at the d.school in Stanford? They have kind of a mindfulness area. Have you seen it?

Malte: No, I haven't seen it!

Miriam: There is this one room with meditation pods hanging from the roof and Yoga mats. I was like – "That's amazing!" I wish we could do that, but we never got it through. And that's the thing maybe and my question to you. I could say that we could do this; integrate mindfulness at the DesignLab and actually role this out for more than just our team with our 35 students and our 28 staff members. When the students approached me a few years ago and said they wanted these sleeping pods and I was not open to the idea I felt – "If you want to sleep, go to your dorm room." In the sense that I was never able to completely understand the added value in integrating this into the rest of DesignLab. I would really love to learn how to...

Malte: To communicate what's your unique selling point or your return on investment, so to say?

Miriam: Yeah, I would really like to get my head around this. On the one hand, I think it is great to cultivate mindfulness and the need to do these things. On the other hand, isn't that something that our sports center on campus does or is it something for which we need a collaboration with the sports center? That DesignLab is not doing these tasks, but we are facilitating the process and the people do it. You know what I mean? We don't want the "label" for the DesignLab that people go there to do mindfulness. But to integrate it into our way of working, create awareness for it and help people to understand what is about, that would be better, right?

Malte: I hear what you say. I mean, as I had quite a deep dive into this topic in the last months, I can tell you that there are some pretty intriguing arguments. One of them is obviously the well-being part. There's now a lot of scientific evidence that mindfulness and meditation practice have very beneficial effects in stressful environments. As you know, I also joined a MBSR course to experience this very systematic and proven approach myself. That's the one thing. However, there is more to it. At the beginning of our conversation, you said that mindfulness and social entrepreneurship are very different things, but there is actually a connection. A researcher who is based in Amsterdam did a very interesting experiment with his colleagues in which he practiced loving-kindness meditation with entrepreneurs and afterwards gave them a business-related decision-making task. He showed that this type of meditation actually supports sustainability-driven decision-making! In addition, practice is catching up. At MIT Sloan, they have the delta v accelerator and recently included a self-awareness program, which also included mindfulness practice. In a survey, over 90% of the participants suggested that self-awareness practice can help entrepreneurs to build more successful businesses. So, the well-being part is very obvious, but there are actually more practical advantages, too.

Miriam: Ok! Well, and I see your point of advocating this topic because sometimes you need to be a front-runner, right? It's also the greatest part of being a part of DesignLab, because we have created this ecosystem where even our executive board boards says – we are the creative ecosystem where we can test things and pilot projects that you cannot try at all other universities, so please be our testing ground for these new ways of working, for innovation and new types of collaboration. That does give us an opportunity!

Malte: I see! I'm so excited that the topic I'm so passionate about found its way into DesignLab already. This also leads me to my last question actually. How do you think Entrepreneurial Mindfulness can become a thing and become a substantial part of ecosystems where people drive change? So that changemakers also take better care of themselves and learn to drive change sustainably. What is missing? What are the roadblocks?

Miriam: I think the roadblocks are the way that people maybe perceive mindfulness. Some people might think it is too far away from their daily practice. I'm going to look at myself here. My first Yoga class was with you and your colleague Sandra-Luisa. Even though it helps a lot, I don't know if it's that I'm scared? Is it too far away from your everyday things? Combining it in a way of working, you have to have people try it! They have to have experienced it and see the value it has added to themselves, but also to the way they approach a challenge. Just like in entrepreneurship. You have to have an added value of mindfulness being a part of entrepreneurship and what it might bring. You said correctly, what the return of investment might be. So if I get my project team at the university to practice mindfulness for a half-hour, what is it going to give me back within my challenge? Do we have statistical numbers that might help people with that? I also believe that we need cheerleaders, innovation hot-spots that do it, like the DesignLab or the d.school. They need to say – "Hey, let's embrace that idea of mindfulness in entrepreneurship and we'd like to be the testing ground to do it." So that you actually have some frontrunners who do it! I don't know, maybe the University of Twente needs to be a testing ground to do that? Here, we have our ecosystem with our incubator Novel-T and DesignLab working together and we could try it in any case. I think you need a proven concept!

Malte: I see your point and I love your enthusiasm! Do you think it would help if I would give a keynote on the topic at DesignLab? To bring it up and get the discussion going?

Miriam: Definitely! Yes, I think we can do that. Also, that's the case with all universities, it helps if we link into what a university has as a goal. For example, our university really wants to work with people, we are the "People first University of Technology", we also would like to work with individuals on social entrepreneurship. If we frame it in a way that links to our university's strategic set of goals and we use this terminology, then people might relate to it a little bit more. Even if it might be a little bit different than what we are usually working on. I would definitely say we could try it together with our incubator Novel-T!

Malte: Cool! That sounds exciting indeed and I'm so up for it! Miriam, thank you so much for your time, feedback and passion for the topic. Let's discuss the details and see how we can make Entrepreneurial Mindfulness a thing together.

## In a Nutshell...

As you can see, Miriam and I are busy making plans already! So if you are reading this book, the University of Twente might well be on the way to becoming the first "cheerleaders" of advocating Entrepreneurial Mindfulness. How cool is that? On a side note, if anyone would ask me how leadership in the 21st century should look like, please have a very close look at what Miriam is doing. Anyway, I learned a few more things in my conversation with her. My Yogi friends will probably not like me for saying that, but there seem to be some open questions about communicating the "added value" of integrating mindfulness and compassion into innovation ecosystems. I don't particularly like it, I didn't decide it to be that way, but being mindful also means to sometimes face uncomfortable truths. What is the return of investment of Entrepreneurial Mindfulness? My personal answer is – more effective changemakers who are living fulfilled and healthy lives and contribute to sustainable economic growth. In this book, I presented supportive evidence and I believe that more evidence will come. Yet, I guess Entrepreneurial Mindfulness advocates will ultimately have to individually convince important stakeholders of their own projects!

We also heard some exciting insights. At DesignLab, an integration of mindfulness practice already began to emerge out of the need to take better care of each other and oneself. Looking at the design thinking process, what better *user insight* could I ask for as an entrepreneur? In this chapter, I mapped out how *actors*, *activities* and *artifacts* might be used to develop mindful innovation ecosystems. Indeed, the DesignLab already discussed meditation pods and experimented with Yoga sessions. However, places in which mindfulness, compassion and driving change fundamentally go hand in hand still seem to be rare to non-existent. I believe that we can do better than that and I am looking for all the cheerleaders out there! Are you an aspiring entrepreneur? Mindfully take your whole self on the journey! Are you an entrepreneur in action? Own your well-being, speak about your troubles and take self-responsibility! Are you a startup coach? Add that five minutes of silence to your coaching session and genuinely ask – "How do you *feel* today?" Are you an investor? Consider well-being metrics for those human beings who are responsible for the sustainability of your investments! Are you an ecosystem builder? Ask for a space of silence and recovery! Are you a researcher? Support Miriam and me with the studies that we need to make our point! We will need all the cheerleaders out there to truly make Entrepreneurial Mindfulness a thing and by now, I don't have any doubt that we should do so. As a last exercise, I want you to manifest your journey into a mindful future. Take what you learned throughout this book and write your own Entrepreneurial Mindfulness manifesto. This world needs you!

# I Dare You:

## Craft Your Entrepreneurial Mindfulness Manifesto!

- Take some time to reflect on the things you learned about global challenges, entrepreneurship, mindfulness and yourself throughout this book
- Start strong – Why does the world need you?
  - Will the world need your innovative ideas and solutions?
  - Will changemakers need your support?
  - Will your decisions stimulate thriving innovation ecosystems?
- Set the hook — Why do you need to integrate more mindfulness and compassion into your work?
  - What are your personal reasons to *mindfully* create the future?
  - Do you always take responsibility for your own well-being?
  - Have you been hard on yourself in the past?
  - Have you been hard on others or have others been hard on you?
- Now what – How will you begin to create the future from the present moment?
  - What will you do to let your light shine?
  - What are the values, attitudes, skills and self-agreements that you will cultivate and live up to?
  - How will you support others in creating the future from the present moment?
- Make it a compelling and vivid piece that you connect with, that keeps you being in peace with yourself and the world around you
- Feel free to share it with the world if you feel comfortable
  - We will need all the cheerleaders and you might well ignite a calming spark of mindfulness and compassion in somebody who really needs this right now!

„As you start to
walk on the way,
the way appears."

RUMI

# Create the Future From This Present Moment

I took you on a journey of Entrepreneurial Mindfulness and why I believe it's worth becoming a thing. Our world will need all the ideas out there to tackle the pressing issues that our society faces. We always relied on creative destroyers, innovative troublemakers and bold entrepreneurs to pave the way into a better future. Yet, society is not asking for a small favor. Startups are built by passion, but there is a catch – a dark side of it. Driving change can be tedious, stressful and it might take its toll on our mental health and well-being! Our minds are not designed for constant *striving* and we need to balance our ambitions with *contentment*. Our mental, physical and social well-being requires us to develop a better understanding of our own human experience, take self-responsibility and appreciate our own boundaries.

Don't get me wrong, I believe that the entrepreneurial journey can be a deeply fulfilling experience and yes, our survival may well depend on the solutions changemakers create for the future. I simply believe that there is a better way of driving change than what is practiced today. Truly living a happy and fulfilled (entrepreneurial) life essentially depends on staying aware of our present moment experience. Yet, understanding and mastering our minds requires dedicated practice. As purpose-driven entrepreneurs, a.k.a. individuals who experience a more extreme version of being human, we will have to find our own, very personal way of navigating this challenge and we should never hesitate to reach out for professional help. Roger, Dagmar, Yuval, Hanna and myself shared our views and experiences and you are welcome to get inspired! These journeys were by no means linear, without setbacks or challenges, but for my part, I can say – It's so worth it!

I hope that in this book, I made my point why we have to create the future from the present moment with mindfulness, compassion and our whole selves. I also hope that I showed that we still have a long way to go in making Entrepreneurial Mindfulness an actual thing. We have to bring it into every corner of the global entrepreneurship community, be it education, training, practice, startups or ecosystems. I also practiced my own creative muscle and showed engaging avenues to take these ideas forward. Feel free to reach out to me if you want to become an Entrepreneurial Mindfulness cheerleader! Yet, this future depends on you, and I can only take you this far on your own journey within. It is time for me to let you take it over. Will you take the next step? Will you deeply inhale the present moment to mindfully exhale a more sustainable and fulfilling future? Will you live up to your manifesto? Just make sure to walk on the way with a trusting heart, your whole self, connected to your purpose, mindful and compassionate. Now, I will let you venture into the unknown with these last words...

May you be well. May you be free from suffering. May you thrive on pursuing your dreams and aspirations. May you find meaningful connections within you and with the world around you. May you be happy and fulfilled.

# My Gratitude

It will be more work than you think. There are many resources for first-time book authors and pretty much all of them agree on this. Of course, I didn't listen... Looking back at the past months, I can genuinely say that I would not have gotten through this on my own. More than once, I had to take a close look at what I was writing about and check in with myself if I stick to it. More often than never, I relied on my sensitive and mindful partner to get me back into the here and now. Thank you, Pia, for your love, your strength and your support for my vision in moments that I needed it most. You are a part of this book beyond the beautiful illustrations that you created. And surely, she is not the only one who left her mark on this book. Without the eye for details of my sister Anna-Lena Krohn, feedback from Steffen Schäfer, Laurie Moore, Jacob Bolton and other early readers, this book would not have been possible. Furthermore, I am grateful for the wisdom of my interviewees Rogelio Arellano, Dagmar Ylva Hattenberg, Yuval Engel, Hanna Tempelhagen and Miriam Iliohan. Also, I thank Hugh Barker for his expert editorial feedback.

I can also say that I could not have gotten to this point in my life on my own. In a way, this book actually started much earlier. There might be some things that I was born with, but many more that I had to learn. Thank you, Birgit, Kay, Angela, Nadine, Anna and Laura for making sure that I embark on my own journey with a feeling of being loved, of being enough, a strong social net and always being provided with everything that I needed. Thank you to my teachers, mentors and the many inspiring people: Merlin Lang, Lucie Beyer, Tobias Welle, Stephan Buse, Cornelius Herstatt, Humera Fasihuddin and the wonderful Faculty Innovation Fellows community, Sean Goldberg, Bente Anderson, Derryn Scott and all my Peaceful Warriors, to name but a few of my heroes. Thank you to the University Innovation Fellows and all the other (yet to become) changemakers. This world needs you!

\* \* \*

While reading this book, you might have noticed that I wrote from different perspectives and in his Book *Incognito*, David Eagleman provides some pretty compelling arguments why this should be the case![56] I have nothing to add to his points. First, reading a book should be like an active collaboration between author and reader. Second, this book is the outcome of many people developing and sharing their knowledge in books, articles and other kinds of publications. Hence, you will often find the narrator's term we instead of *I*.

Inhale the present.
Exhale the future.

# Notes

Works listed in full in the Bibliography are referred to with author name or publishing institution, year of publication and page number here.

Embarking on Our Journey

**1** See Ries (2011).

**2** See Jacob, Jovic and Brinkerhoff (2009).

**3** See García and Miralles (2017).

**4** Japanologist Nicholas Kemp discussed why the original Japanese concept of Ikigai is not best represented by the Venn Diagram in a well-written blog article (Kemp, 2020).

**5** Andrés Chinchilla and Mayte Garcia discuss the duality of objectives inherent to social entrepreneurship and how this relates to mindfulness (Chinchilla & Garcia, 2017).

**6** Eva de Mol and her colleagues conducted a study on entrepreneurial burnout and showed that entrepreneurs who are obsessively passionate about their entrepreneurial identity are more likely to experience burnout (De Mol, Ho, & Pollack, 2018).

**7** Yuval Engel and colleagues argue that entrepreneurial success is not only a function of effectively navigating the business environment, but also effectively dealing with the inner challenges (Engel et al., 2019).

Part One – A Threefold Challenge

**1** See Chinchilla and Garcia (2017).

**2** See Note 1.

**3** See Engel et al. (2019).

**4** See Schumpeter (1939).

**5** The other trends discussed by EY are Digital Future, Global Marketplace Urban World, Resourceful Planet and Health Reimagined (ERNST & YOUNG, 2015)

**6** See United Nations (2020).

**7** See von Hippel (2006).

**8** See Herstatt and von Hippel (1992).

**9** See von Hippel (2016).

**10** See e.g. Thompson, Kiefer and York (2011) for a discussion about the distinctiveness of social, sustainable and environmental entrepreneurship.

**11** Just check out his Twitter (Musk, 2019).

**12** Read more about precious plastic's story on their *About* section (Precious Plastic, 2020).

**13** You can find all the information on Susanne's website (Circular Thinking, 2020).

**14** See Dweck (2012).

**15** See Blackwell, Trzesniewski and Dweck (2007) and Yeager et al. (2019).

**16** See Schumpeter (1939, p. 148).

**17** See e.g. Dillon (2011).

**18** See Griffin (1997).

**19** You can find a discussion about the "urban legend" of product failures in Castellion and Markham (2013).

**20** See Ries (2011).

**21** See Osterwalder (2004).

**22** See Bland and Osterwalder (2019).

**23** See Osterwalder and Pigneur (2010).

**24** See WHO (1948, p. 1).

**25** See CDC (2018).

**26** See Frankl (2008)

**27** See Stephan (2018).

**28** See Topp et al. (2015).

**29** See Thompson, van Gelderen and Keppler (2020) for a recent study how entrepreneurs cope with the fear of failure.

**30** Wiklund et al. (2019) published a special issue on entrepreneurial well-being in the Journal of Business Venturing.

**31** See Stephan (2018) for a review of entrepreneurial well-being and mental health.

**32** See Muenster and Hokemeyer (2019). They refer to an earlier version of Freeman et al. (2019).

**33** See Freeman et al. (2019).

**34** See de Mol, Ho and Pollack (2018).

**35** See Shir and Ryff (2021).

**36** See Kabat-Zinn (2009, pp. 5-6)

Part Two – The Entrepreneurial Journey

**1** See Carlsson et al. (2013, p. 914). CC BY License.

**2** See Krueger (2003) for a seminal discussion of important concepts and research directions. Especially intention research in entrepreneurship was sparked by Norris Krueger's ideas.

**3** See e.g. Hattenberg, Belousova and Groen (2020).

**4** See Krohn et al. (2021).

**5** See Gollwitzer (1990)

**6** See Gollwitzer and Sheeran (2006) for a review of empirical studies building on implementation intentions.

**7** See Clear (2018).

**8** Delanoë-Gueguen and Fayolle (2019) discuss two distinct types of mindsets. The original work of Gollwiter and newer publications also include an actional as well as evaluative mindset (Achtziger & Gollwitzer, 2018). For reasons of simplicity, I present this version.

**9** See Delanoë-Gueguen and Fayolle (2019).

**10** See Krueger (2007b, p. 123).

**11** See Shepherd, Patzelt and Haynie (2010).

**12** See Shepherd, Patzelt and Haynie (2010, p. 62).

**13** See TOMS (2019).

**14** See Too Good To Go (2020).

**15** See Krueger (2007a).

**16** On 2020/12/21 the citation count on Google Scholar for Icek Ajzen was 342.570 and for Richard Thaler 158.003.

**17** See Ajzen (1991).

**18** See Burnette et al. (2020).

**19** See Kautonen, van Gelderen and Tornikoski (2013)

**20** See Csikszentmihalyi (1990).

**21** See McKnight and Kashdan (2009). The discussion of purpose in this section is mainly based on their conceptual model.

**22** They refer to Brown, Ryan and Creswel's (2007) review of the theoretical foundations of mindfulness.

**23** See Note 21.

**24** See Hockerts (2006).

**25** See García and Miralles (2017).

**26** See Kemp (2020).

**27** See Kabat-Zinn (2009, p. 76).

Part Three – Infusing Mindfulness

**1** Yuval Engel and colleagues showed that loving-kindness meditations contribute to entrepreneurs sustainable decision making (Engel, Ramesh, & Steiner, 2020). Yuval Engel and colleagues also show that loving-kindness meditation reduces entrepreneurial fear of failure, which might be related to negative mental health outcomes (Engel, et al., 2019). Yuval Engel also brought up the idea of improved decision-making in our Deep Dive. Furthermore, Marco van Gelderen and colleagues suggest that mindful individuals make more ethical entrepreneurial decisions (Van Gelderen, et al., 2019). Louise Kelly and Marina Dorian conceptually explore the role of mindfulness in the entrepreneurial opportunity recognition process and propose similar relationships like this book (Kelly & Dorian, 2017).

**2** See Cadwalladr (2015).

**3** See Kabat-Zinn (1982).

**4** See the study of Jenny Gu and colleagues for a review of mindfulness effects and mechanisms (Gu, et al., 2015).

**5** See Brown and Ryan (2003) as discussed in Brown, Ryan and Creswell (2007, p. 212).

**6** In Brown and Ryan (2003) you will find the published and validated scale. However, there are other publicly available versions.

**7** See Shapiro et al. (2008).

**8** See Chatzisarantis and Hagger (2007).

**9** See van Gelderen et al. (2019).

**10** See Engel, Ramesh and Steiner (2020).

**11** See Ruedy and Schweitzer (2010).

**12** See Karelaia and Reb (2015).

**13** See Good et al. (2016).

**14** Two recent reviews on the topic agree on the distinctive context of entrepreneurs (Stephan, 2018; Wiklund, et al., 2019).

**15** See Engel et al. (2019).

**16** E.g. Rivoallan (2018) or Freeman et al. (2019).

**17** See Kabat-Zinn J. (2009).

**Quote** by Osho (2012).

**18** Brown and Ryan (2003) as discussed in Brown, Ryan and Creswell (2007, p. 212).

**19** See Kabat-Zinn and Hanh (2009).

**20** See van Gelderen et al. (2019).

**21** See Lyddy and Good (2017). In the remainder of this chapter, I refer to this study when mentioning Lyddy and Good, being, doing or being-while-doing.

**22** As discussed by van Gelderen et al. (2019), Marco van Gelderen and colleagues propose a mode of Being-while-Striving in the context of entrepreneurship. However, this is rather a future research proposition. The authors do not go into detail about the mode of striving and it's distinctiveness from doing.

**23** See Delanoë-Gueguen and Fayolle (2019).

**24** See van Gelderen et al. (2019).

**25** See Kabat-Zinn (1982).

**26** See Gu et al. (2015).

**27** See Kabat-Zinn and Hanh (2009).

**28** See Brown and Ryan (2003).

**29** See Topp et al. (2015).

**30** See Brown and Ryan (2003).

**31** See Note 29.

**32** See Note 29.

**33** See Lyddy and Good (2017).

Part Four – Entrepreneurial Mindfulness

**1** This paragraph is based on the findings of David Erler's study, which David as the main author and me currently prepare for publication. Before he did 36 interviews at Hamburg University of Technology and the University of Twente, he conducted a comprehensive literature review to develop a conceptual basis.

**2** See Gollwitzer (2012, p. 526).

**3** See Delanoë-Gueguen and Fayolle (2019).

**4** See e.g. Shirokova, Tsukanova and Morris (2018), Lüthje and Franke (2004) or Bae et al. (2014).

**5** See Fayolle et al. (2006).

**6** See Daniel (2016).

**7** See Liñán, Rodriguez-Cohard and Rueda-Cantuche (2011).

**8** See Naumann (2017).

**9** See Delanoë-Gueguen and Fayolle (2019).

**10** See Note 9.

**11** See Achtziger and Gollwitzer (2018).

**12** See Delanoë-Gueguen and Fayolle (2019).

**13** See Kuratko, Fisher and Audretsch (2020).

**14** See Engel, Ramesh and Steiner (2020).

**15** See van Gelderen et al. (2019).

**16** See Gu et al. (2015).

**17** See Engel et al. (2019).

**18** See MIT Sloan (2019).

**19** See Burnette et al. (2020).

**20** See e.g. Brown (2008).

**21** See Daniel (2016).

**22** See Leppma and Young (2016).

**23** See Galla et al. (2016).

**24** See Good et al. (2016).

**25** See van Gelderen et al. (2019).

**26** See Good et al. (2016).

**27** See Frijda (1988).

**28** See Gilbert (2009).

**29** See Freeman et al. (2019).

**30** See Engel et al. (2019).

**31** See Gilbert (2009).

**32** See Gotink et al. (2016) for a review.

**33** Find a respective definition in Goetz, Keltner and Simon-Thomas (2010).

**34** See Neff (2003).

**35** See Engel et al. (2019).

**36** See Gilbert (2009, p. 277).

**37** See Good et al. (2016).

**38** For example, Krohn et al. (2021) present recent conceptual work, integrating different mindset-based perspectives with innovation and entrepreneurship.

**39** See de Mol, Ho and Pollack (2018).

**Quote** by Kornfield (2017) with kind permission from Jack Kornfield.

**40** See Granstrand and Holgersson (2020).

**41** See Jansen et al. (2015).

**42** See Barrett et al. (2015).

**43** See Wright, Siegel and Mustar (2017).

**44** See Universiteit Twente (2021a).

**45** See Universiteit Twente (2021b).

**46** See UniversiteitTwente (2021c).

**47** See Universiteit Twente (2021b).

**48** See IDEO (2021).

**49** See Brenner, Uebernickel and Abrell (2016).

**50** The d.school shares many useful resources to understand and apply their approach to design thinking (Doorley et al., 2018).

**51** See Savoia (2019).

**52** See Good et al. (2016, p. 135).

**53** Brené Brown's book on the importance of vulnerability was one of my favorite reads in 2020 and I highly recommend it to everybody who believes that there must be better ways to live, work and connect with one another (Brown, 2015).

**54** See MIT Sloan (2019).

**55** See Delizonna (2017).

**56** See Eagleman (2012, p. 228).

# Bibliography

Achtziger, A., & Gollwitzer, P. (2018). Motivation and Volition in the Course of Action. In *Motivation and Action* (3 ed., pp. 485–527). Cham: Springer International Publishing.

Ajzen, I. (1991). The Theory of Planned Behavior. *Organizational Behavior and Human Decision Processes, 50*(2), pp. 179–211.

Bae, T., Qian, S., Miao, C., & Fiet, J. (2014). The Relationship Between Entrepreneurship Education and Entrepreneurial Intentions: A Meta-Analytic Review. *Entrepreneurship Theory and Practice, 38*(2), 217–254.

Barrett, T., Pizzico, M., Levy, B., Nagel, R., Linsey, J., Talley, K., . . . Newstetter, W. (2015). A Review of University Maker Spaces. *ASEE Annual Conference and Exposition, Conference Proceedings, Vol. 122.*

Blackwell, L. S., Trzesniewski, K. H., & Dweck, C. S. (2007). Implicit Theories Of Intelligence Predict Achievement Across an Adolescent Transition: A longitudinal Study and an Intervention. *Child Development, 78*(1), 246-263.

Bland, D. J., & Osterwalder, A. (2019). *Testing Business Ideas: A Field Guide for Rapid Experimentation.* Hoboken: John Wiley & Sons.

Brenner, W., Uebernickel, F., & Abrell, T. (2016). Design Thinking as Mindset, Process, and Toolbox. In *Design thinking for Innovation* (pp. 3-21). Springer, Cham.

Brown, B. (2015). *Daring Greatly: How the Courage to be Vulnerable Transforms the Way We Live, Love, Parent, and Lead.* UK: Penguin.

Brown, K. W., & Ryan, R. M. (2003). The Benefits of Being Present: Mindfulness and its Role in Psychological Well-Being. *Journal of Personality and Social Psychology, 84*(4), 822.

Brown, K. W., Ryan, R. M., & Creswell, J. D. (2007). Mindfulness: Theoretical Foundations and Evidence for its Salutary effects. *Psychological Inquiry, 18*(4), 211-237.

Brown, T. (2008). Design thinking. *Harvard Business Review, 86*(6), 84-94.

Burnette, J. L., Pollack, J. M., Forsyth, R. B., Hoyt, C. L., Thomas, F. N., & Coy, A. E. (2020). A Growth Mindset Intervention: Enhancing Students' Entrepreneurial Self-Efficacy and Career Development. *Entrepreneurship Theory and Practice, 44*(5), 878-908.

Cadwalladr, C. (2015). *Yuval Noah Harari: The age of the Cyborg has Begun – and the Consequences Cannot be Known*. Retrieved 12 27, 2020, from The Guardian: https://www.theguardian.com/culture/2015/jul/05/yuval-harari-sapiens-interview-age-of-cyborgs

Carlsson, B., Braunerhjelm, P., McKelvey, M., Olofsson, C., Persson, L., & Ylinenpää, H. (2013). The Evolving Domain of Entrepreneurship Research. *Small Business Economics, 41*(4), 913-930.

Castellion, G., & Markham, S. K. (2013). Perspective: New Product Failure Rates: Influence of Argumentum ad Populum and Self-Interest. *Journal of Product Innovation Management, 30*(5), 976-979.

CDC. (2018). *Well-Being Concepts*. Retrieved 12 15, 2020, from Center for Desease Control and Prevention: https://www.cdc.gov/hrqol/wellbeing.htm

Chatzisarantis, N. L., & Hagger, M. S. (2007). Mindfulness and the Intention-behavior Relationship Within the Theory of Planned Behavior. *Personality and Social Psychology Bulletin, 33*(5), 663-676.

Chinchilla, A., & Garcia, M. (2017). Social Entrepreneurship Intention: Mindfulness Towards a Duality of Objectives. *Humanistic Management Journal, 1*(2), 205-214.

Circular Thinking. (2020). Retrieved 12 13, 2020, from Circular Thinking: https://en.circular-thinking.net/

Clear, J. (2018). *Atomic Habits: An Easy & Proven Way to Build Good Habits & Break Bad Ones*. USA: Penguin Random House.

Csikszentmihalyi, M. (1990). *Flow: The psychology of Optimal Experience*. New York: Harper & Row.

Daniel, A. (2016). Fostering an Entrepreneurial Mindset by Using a Design Thinking Approach in Entrepreneurship Education. *Industry and Higher Education, 30*(3), 215–223.

De Mol, E., Ho, V. T., & Pollack, J. M. (2018). Predicting Entrepreneurial Burnout in a Moderated Mediated Model of Job Fit. *Journal of Small Business Management, 56*(3), 392-411.

Delanoë-Gueguen, S., & Fayolle, A. (2019). Crossing the Entrepreneurial Rubicon: A Longitudinal Investigation. *Journal of Small Business Management, 57*(3), 1044-1065.

Delizonna, L. (2017). High-Performing Teams Need Psychological Safety. Here's How to Create It. *Harvard Business Review, 24*, 1-5.

Dillon, K. (2011). I Think of My Failures as a Gift. *Harvard Business Review, 89*(4), 69-74.

Doorley, S., Holcomb, S., Klebahn, P., Segovia, K. & Utley, J. (2018). *Design Thinking Bootleg*. Retrieved 02 11, 2021, from d.school Stanford: https://dschool.stanford.edu/resources/design-thinking-bootleg

Dweck, C. (2012). *Mindset: Changing the Way You Think to Fulfil Your Potential*. London: Hachette UK.

Eagleman, D. (2012). *Incognito: The Secret Lives of the Brain*. USA: Vintage Books.

Engel, Y., Noordijk, S., Spoelder, A., & van Gelderen, M. (2019). Self-compassion when Coping With Venture Obstacles: Loving-kindness Meditation and Entrepreneurial Fear of Failure. *Entrepreneurship Theory and Practice, 45*(2), 263–290.

Engel, Y., Ramesh, A., & Steiner, N. (2020). Powered by Compassion: The Effect of Loving-kindness Meditation on Entrepreneurs' Sustainable Decision-making. *Journal of Business Venturing, 35*(6), 105986.

ERNST & YOUNG. (2015). *Megatrends 2015 Making Sense of a World in Motion*. Retrieved 08 23, 2020, from https://www.ey.com/Publication/vwLUAssets/ey-megatrends-report-2015/$FILE/ey-megatrends-report-2015.pdf

Fayolle, A., Gailly, B., & Lassas-Clerc, N. (2006). Assessing the Impact of Entrepreneurship Education Programmes: A New Methodology. *Journal of European Industrial Training, 30*(9), 701-720.

Frankl, V. E. (2008). *Man's Search for Meaning: The Classic Tribute to Hope from the Holocaust*. UK: Rider.

Freeman, M. A., Staudenmaier, P. J., Zisser, M. R., & Andresen, L. A. (2019). The Prevalence and Co-occurrence of Psychiatric Conditions Among Entrepreneurs and Their Families. *Small Business Economics, 53*(2), 323-342.

Frijda, N. H. (1988). The Laws of Emotion. *American Psychologist, 43*(5), 349-358.

Galla, B. M., Baelen, R. N., Duckworth, A. L., & Baime, M. J. (2016). Mindfulness, Meet Self-regulation: Boosting Out-of-class Meditation Practice with Brief Action Plans. *Motivation Science, 2*(4), 220-237.

García, H., & Miralles, F. (2017). *Ikigai: The Japanese Secret to a Long and Happy Life*. London: Penguin.

Gilbert, P. (2009). *The Compassionate Mind*. London: Robinson.

Goetz, J. L., Keltner, D., & Simon-Thomas, E. (2010). Compassion: An Evolutionary Analysis and Empirical Review. *Psychological Bulletin, 136*(3), 351-374.

Gollwitzer, P. (2012). Mindset Theory of Action Phases. In *Handbook of Theories of Social Psychology* (pp. 526–545). Los Angeles: Sage Publications.

Gollwitzer, P. M. (1990). Action Phases and Mind-sets. In *Handbook of Motivation and Cognition: Foundations of Social Behavior* (2 ed., pp. 53-92). United Kingdom: Guilford Press.

Gollwitzer, P. M., & Sheeran, P. (2006). Implementation Intentions and Goal Achievement: A Meta-analysis of Effects and Processes. *Advances in Experimental Social Psychology, 38*, 69-119.

Good, D. J., Lyddy, C. J., Glomb, T. M., Bono, J. E., Brown, K. W., Duffy, M. K., . . . Lazar, S. W. (2016). Contemplating Mindfulness at Work: An Integrative Review. *Journal of Management, 42*(1), 114-142.

Gotink, R. A., Meijboom, R., Vernooij, M. W., & Hunink, M. M. (2016). 8-week Mindfulness Based Stress Reduction Induces Brain Changes Similar to Traditional Long-term Meditation Practice – A Systematic Review. *Brain and Cognition, 108*, 32-41.

Granstrand, O., & Holgersson, M. (2020). Innovation Ecosystems: A Conceptual Review and a New Definition. *Technovation, 90-91*, 102098.

Griffin, A. (1997). PDMA Research on New Product Development Practices: Updating Trends and Benchmarking Best Practices. *Journal of Product Innovation Management: An International Publication of The Product Development & Management Association, 14*(6), 429.

Gu, J., Strauss, C., Bond, R., & Cavanagh, K. (2015). How do Mindfulness-based Cognitive Therapy and Mindfulness-based Stress Reduction Improve Mental Health and Wellbeing? A Systematic Review and Meta-analysis of Mediation Studies. *Clinical Psychology Review, 37*, 1-12.

Hattenberg, D., Belousova, O., & Groen, A. (2020). Defining the Entrepreneurial Mindset and Discussing its Distinctiveness in Entrepreneurship Research. *International Journal of Entrepreneurship and Small Business*.

Herstatt, C., & Von Hippel, E. (1992). From Experience: Developing New Product Concepts via the Lead User Method: A Case Study in a "Low-tech" Field. *Journal of Product Innovation Management, 9*(3), 213-221.

Hockerts, K. (2006). Entrepreneurial Opportunity in Social Purpose Business Ventures. In *Social entrepreneurship* (pp. 142-154). London: Palgrave Macmillan.

IDEO (2021). *Design Thinking*. Retrieved 02 11, 2021, from IDEO: https://designthinking.ideo.com/

Jacob, J., Jovic, E., & Brinkerhoff, M. B. (2009). Personal and Planetary Well-being: Mindfulness Meditation, Pro-environmental Behavior and Personal Quality of Life in a Survey From the Social Justice and Ecological Sustainability Movement. *Social Indicators Research, 93*(2), 275-294.

Jansen, S., van de Zande, T., Brinkkemper, S. E., & Varma, V. (. (2015). How Education, Stimulation, and Incubation Encourage Student Entrepreneurship: Observations from MIT, IIIT, and Utrecht University. *The International Journal of Management Education, 13*(2), 170–181.

Kabat-Zinn, J. (1982). An Outpatient Program in Behavioral Medicine for Chronic Pain Patients Based on the Practice of Mindfulness Meditation: Theoretical Considerations and Preliminary Results. *General Hospital Psychiatry, 4*(1), 33-47.

Kabat-Zinn, J. (2009). *Wherever You Go, There You Are: Mindfulness Meditation in Everyday Life.* London: Hachette Books.

Kabat-Zinn, J., & Hanh, T. N. (2009). *Full Catastrophe Ilving: Using the Wisdom of Your Body and Mind to Face Stress, Pain, and Illness.* New York, New York: Delta.

Karelaia, N., & Reb, J. (2015). Improving Decision Making Through Mindfulness. In *Mindfulness in organizations: Foundations, research, and applications* (pp. 256-284). Cambridge University Press.

Kautonen, T., van Gelderen, M., & Tornikoski, E. T. (2013). Predicting Entrepreneurial Behaviour: A Test of the Theory of Planned Behaviour. *Applied Economics, 45*(6), 697-707.

Kelly, L., & Dorian, M. (2017). Doing Well and Good: An Exploration of the Role of Mindfulness in the Entrepreneurial Opportunity Recognition and Evaluation Process. *New England Journal of Entrepreneurship, 20*(2), 25-35.

Kemp, N. (2020). *Ikigai Is Not a Venn Diagram.* Retrieved 09 29, 2020, from Medium: https://ikigaitribe.medium.com/ikigai-is-not-a-venn-diagram-cca7abba323

Kornfield, J. (2017). *No Time Like the Present: Finding Freedom, Love, and Joy Right Where You Are.* USA: Atria Books.

Krohn, M., Hattenberg, D., Krueger, N., & Herstatt, C. (2021). A Taxonomy of Mindsets — Unlocking the Synergy of Innovation and Entrepreneurship through Mindset-Based Perspectives. *28th IPDMC: Innovation and Product Development Management Conference.* Milan, Italy.

Krueger, N. (2007a). The Cognitive Infrastructure of Opportunity Emergence. In *Entrepreneurship* (pp. 185-206). Berlin, Heidelberg: Springer.

Krueger, N. (2007b). What Lies Beneath? The Experiential Essence of Entrepreneurial Thinking. *Entrepreneurship Theory and Practice, 31*(1), 123–138.

Krueger, N. F. (2003). The Cognitive Psychology of Entrepreneurship. In *Handbook of entrepreneurship research* (pp. 105-140). Boston, MA: Springer.

Kuratko, D. F., Fisher, G., & Audretsch, D. B. (2020). Unraveling the Entrepreneurial Mindset. Small Business Economics. https://doi.org/10.1007/s11187-020-00372-6.

Leppma, M., & Young, M. E. (2016). Loving-kindness Meditation and Empathy: A Wellness Group Intervention for Counseling Students. *Journal of Counseling & Development, 94*(3), 297-305.

Liñán, F., Rodriguez-Cohard, J., & Rueda-Cantuche, J. (2011). Factors Affecting Entrepreneurial Intention Levels: A Role for education. *International Entrepreneurship and Management Journal, 7*(2), 195–218.

Lüthje, C., & Franke, N. (2004). Entrepreneurial Intentions of Business Students:. A Benchmarking Study. *International Journal of Innovation and Technology Management, 1*(3), 269–288.

Lyddy, C. J., & Good, D. J. (2017). Being While Doing: An Inductive Model of Mindfulness at Work. *Frontiers in Psychology, 7*:2060, https://doi.org/10.3389/fpsyg.2016.02060.

McKnight, P. E., & Kashdan, T. B. (2009). Purpose in Life as a System That Creates and Sustains Health and Well-being: An Integrative, Testable Theory. *Review of General Psychology, 13*(3), 242-251.

MIT Sloan. (2019). *MIT Sloan Accelerator Announces Results of First Self-awareness Program for Entrepreneurs.* Retrieved 01 16, 2021, from MIT Sloan: https://mitsloan.mit.edu/press/mit-sloan-accelerator-announces-results-first-self-awareness-program-entrepreneurs

Muenster, M., & Hokemeyer, P. (2019). *There is a Mental Health Crisis in Entrepreneurship. Here's How to Tackle it.* Retrieved 12 18, 2020, from World Economic Forum: https://www.weforum.org/agenda/2019/03/how-to-tackle-the-mental-health-crisis-in-entrepreneurship/

Musk, E. (2019). *Elon Musk.* Retrieved 12 13, 2020, from Twitter: https://twitter.com/elonmusk/status/1091077858947035136

Naumann, C. (2017). Entrepreneurial Mindset: A Synthetic Literature Review. *Entrepreneurial Business and Economics Review, 5*(3), 149–172.

Neff, K. (2003). Self-compassion: An Alternative Conceptualization of a Healthy Attitude Toward Oneself. *Self and Identity, 2*(2), 85-101.

Osho. (2012). *The Mind: a Beautiful Servant, a Dangerous Master.* Osho Media International.

Osterwalder, A. (2004). *The Business Model Ontology: A Proposition in a Design Science Approach.* Doctoral dissertation, Université de Lausanne, Faculté des hautes études commerciales.

Osterwalder, A., & Pigneur, Y. (2010). *Business Model Generation: A Handbook for Visionaries, Game*

*Changers, and Challengers*. Hoboken: John Wiley & Sons.

Precious Plastic. (2020). *History*. Retrieved 12 13, 2020, from Precious Plastic: https://preciousplastic.com/about/history.html

Ries, E. (2011). *The Lean Startup: How Today's Entrepreneurs Use Continuous Innovation to Create Radically Successful Businesses*. USA: Currency.

Rivoallan, G. (2018). The Role of Mindfulness in the Development of Resilience in Entrepreneurs. *Doctoral Dissertation, Sheffield Hallam University*.

Ruedy, N. E., & Schweitzer, M. E. (2010). In the Moment: The Effect of Mindfulness on Ethical Decision making. *Journal of Business Ethics, 95*(1), 73-87.

Savoia, A. (2019). *The Right It: Why so Many Ideas Fail and How to Make Sure Yours Succeed*. New York: HarperCollins.

Schumpeter, J. A. (1939). *Business Cycles*. New York: McGraw-Hill.

Shapiro, S. L., Oman, D., Thoresen, C. E., Plante, T. G., & Flinders, T. (2008). Cultivating Mindfulness: Effects on Well-being. *Journal of Clinical Psychology, 64*(7), 840-862.

Shepherd, D., Patzelt, H., & Haynie, J. (2010). Entrepreneurial Spirals: Deviation-amplifying Loops of an Entrepreneurial Mindset and Organizational Culture. *Entrepreneurship Theory and Practice, 34*(1), 59-82.

Shir, N., & Ryff, C. D. (2021). Entrepreneurship, Self-Organization, and Eudaimonic Well-Being: A Dynamic Approach. *Entrepreneurship Theory and Practice*. https://doi.org/10.1177/10422587211013798.

Shirokova, G., Tsukanova, T., & Morris, M. (2018). The Moderating Role of National Culture in the Relationship Between University Entrepreneurship Offerings and Student Start-Up Activity: An Embeddedness Perspective. *Journal of Small Business Management, 56*(1), 103–130.

Stephan, U. (2018). Entrepreneurs' Mental Health and Well-being: A Review and Research Agenda. *Academy of Management Perspectives, 32*(3), 290-322.

Strategyzer AG. (2021). *Business Model Canvas*. Retrieved 12 15, 2020, from Strategyzer AG: https://www.strategyzer.com/canvas/business-model-canvas

Thompson, N. A., van Gelderen, M., & Keppler, L. (2020). No Need to Worry? Anxiety and Coping in the Entrepreneurship Process. *Frontiers in Psychology, 11:389*, https://doi.org/10.3389/

fpsyg.2020.00398.

Thompson, N., Kiefer, K., & York, J. G. (2011). Distinctions not Dichotomies: Exploring Social, Ssustainable, and Environmental Entrepreneurship. In *Social and sustainable entrepreneurship* (pp. 205–233). Bingley: Emerald Group Publishing Limited.

TOMS. (2019). *Impact.* Retrieved 12 21, 2020, from TOMS Shoes: https://www.toms.com/us/impact.html

Too Good To Go. (2020). *Movement.* Retrieved 12 21, 2020, from Too Good To Go: https://toogoodtogo.com/en-us/movement

Topp, C. W., Østergaard, S. D., Søndergaard, S., & Bech, P. (2015). The WHO-5 Well-Being Index: A Systematic Review of the Literature. *Psychotherapy and Psychosomatics, 84*(3), 167-176.

United Nations. (2020). *The Sustainable Development Goals Report.* Retrieved 12 12, 2020, from United Nations: https://unstats.un.org/sdgs/report/2020/

Universiteit Twente. (2021a). *Support for Startups.* Retrieved 02 01, 2021, from Universiteit Twente: https://www.utwente.nl/en/business/support-for-start-ups/

Universiteit Twente. (2021b). *DesignLab Organization.* Retrieved 02 04, 2021, from Universiteit Twente: https://www.utwente.nl/en/designlab/organisation/

UniversiteitTwente. (2021c). *DesignLab.* Retrieved 02 11, 2021, from Universiteit Twente: https://www.utwente.nl/en/designlab/

Van Gelderen, M., Kibler, E., Kautonen, T., Munoz, P., & Wincent, J. (2019). Mindfulness and Taking Action to Start a New Business. *Journal of Small Business Management, 57*(S2), 489-506.

Von Hippel, E. (2006). *Democratizing Innovation.* Cambridge, London: The MIT Press.

Von Hippel, E. (2016). *Free innovation.* Cambridge, London: The MIT Press.

WHO. (1948). *Constitution.* Retrieved 12 15, 2020, from World Health Organization: https://www.who.int/about/who-we-are/constitution

Wiklund, J., Nikolaev, B., Shir, N., Foo, M. D., & Bradley, S. (2019). Entrepreneurship and Well-being: Past, Present, and Future. *Journal of Business Venturing, 34*(4), 579-588.

Wright, M., Siegel, D., & Mustar, P. (2017). An Emerging Ecosystem for Student Start-ups. *The Journal of Technology Transfer, 42*(4), 909–922.

Yeager, D. S., Walton, G. M., Murray, J. S., Crosnoe, R., Muller, C., ..., & Dweck, C. S. (2019). A National Experiment Reveals Where a Growth Mindset Improves Achievement. *Nature, 573*(7774), 364-369.

# Index

9 783000 701726